Qanon And The Dark Agenda
The Illuminati Protocols Exposed

Michael Knight

Copyright © June 2020 North Star Publishing Inc

All rights reserved

No part of this book may be reproduced, or stored in a retrieval system, or transmitted in any form or by any means, electronic, mechanical, photocopying, recording, or otherwise, without express written permission of the publisher, except for excerpts as per the Fair Use Clause of the US Copyright Act, with full credit and link back to the author's website.

ISBN-13: 978-1-7340837-4-3

COPYRIGHT FAIR USE

Where reference is made to what may be copyright material and sources, including the use of excerpts therefrom, relevant credit and links are provided. Such use complies with the Fair Use clause of the Copyright Law of the United States. Title 17 of the United States Code 107. Limitations on exclusive rights: Fair use ".... the fair use of a copyrighted work ... for purposes such as criticism, comment, news reporting, teaching ... scholarship, or research, is not an infringement of copyright." Government publications and transcripts are not subject to copyright and therefore may be used in full.

ACKNOWLEDGMENTS

Cover Art https://selfpubbookcovers.com/RLSather

Cover Text And Layout Sherrie St. James Studios
Professional Graphic Design & Photography
SherrieStJames@gmail.com

Proof Reading/Copy Editing Victoria Blaze

DEDICATION

In memory of my father, Hector William Knight, who as an armorer in the Royal New Zealand Air Force was deployed to Green Island and Guadalcanal in the Pacific to assist the US victory in the Second World War. Little did he know that 75 years later America would once again be under assault, not by invasion but by infiltration and an enemy within.

CONTENTS

Title Page
Copyright
Copyright Fair Use
Acknowledgments
Dedication
Introduction   2
What IS Qanon?   8
Serge Monast – R.I.P.   13
The Toronto Protocols   15
6.6.6. Bucket List   21
Conspiracy Theories   24
Real Fake News   27
Project Mockingbird   29
Good Unmasking Bad   33
Spies For China   47
Two Dark Agendas   51
Obama's Agenda   53
Hillary's Agenda   54
We Avoided WW3   55
The Obama Record   57

Deep State Runs Deep	61
Uranium One	64
How They Do It	67
Research Exercise	68
Chemtrails	73
Death and Denial	77
Killer Chemicals	81
Monsanto	83
GMO Suicides	86
Triffids and Ovens	87
DARPA = FB = DS	89
Election Fraud	91
Education – Obama $$$	95
Trading Children	99
Executive Order 138128	107
Clinton Connection?	109
US Trafficking	111
The Red Dawn – 1985	115
God Wins!	122
Black Hats - Black Budgets	127
Silent Weapons	129
Rockefeller Scenarios	133
Q Goes Global	140
Macron – Globalist	143
Yellow Vests	147
Mind Control	150
The New Sheriff	155
2017 UN Speech	158

B.O. – Unforgiven	175
Putin – Anti NWO?	177
SOTU 2018	181
SOTU Speech	184
Assassination	203
2018 UN Speech	207
About Trump	221
Research 101	236
Top Sites	243
Research Q	246
Recommended Videos	250
MK Books And Videos	252
Reviews – Please	254
About The Author	255
Contact Michael Knight	258
Addendum – The Virus Speaks	259

MICHAEL KNIGHT

INTRODUCTION

A Note From The Author.

First things first. I have been researching, learning and writing about those I call the Globalists for decades.

This knowledge has certainly been enhanced by reading and researching Internet posts by an entity known as Q. However, I have not participated in any of the Qanon forums, simply because as an honest reporter, in order to ensure objectivity I have never joined any political party or group.

Nevertheless, having observed the Qanon posts and discussions since 2017, it has become very clear to me that what the mainstream media describes as a far out conspiracy theory, is anything but.

I don't expect you to take my word for it, but it seems to me that this Qanon movement may well be the best last chance the world has to get out from under the deeply entrenched control of a few family dynasties and their few thousand lackeys.

You may very well come to a similar conclusion, but the choice is always yours.

Authoring a book such as this is quite different from simply reporting what others have to say.
Consequently, it includes many of my personal opinions and assessments of what I refer to as The Dark Agenda. I have done my

best to accurately paint "the Big Picture," but only as a starting point; as informative as it is, this book should only be seen as a springboard from which to do further research to broaden your own knowledge base.

I wrote this book as if I were talking to you in person. However, I am not a literary purist. My writing "voice" stems from decades working in radio and television, where sentences are constructed to be read aloud. That's how this book is written because at some point it will become an audio book as well.

In addition, even though my file statistics tell me this manuscript has taken 271 hours to complete, along with 270 revisions, you'll probably still find a few typos and punctuation errors, and that I break some rules relating to sentence construction.

That said, in this book I do my best to write for those who are willing to risk thinking outside the box to look into the darker side of things, such as the role of what is known these days as the Deep State.

They have also been known as the Illuminati, the Cabal, and as Khazarians. Their common goal is the establishment of a New World Order wherein we are controlled by a world government, a world religion, a world court and other institutions whose only purpose would be to completely control our lives.

There would no longer be individual sovereign nations.
America as the Founding Fathers intended it to be – a unique Republic in which the people control the government - would cease to exist.

This book reveals how they have planned to achieve that objective – and what is now being done by way of both information warfare and a silent but very real battle behind the scenes to stop their global takeover.

My contribution here is through using such skills and knowledge as I acquired in a career as an honest investigative reporter, including an awareness of the New World Order agenda starting in the 1970s.

On that subject, I wrote and published *President Trump and the New World Order* in September 2017, a month before Q and the Qanons came on the scene.

Naturally, as far as this "Q" thing was concerned, I was intrigued, initially skeptical, and cautious. However, after keeping an eye on the many Posts Q made in the following six months, and seeing what are now recognized as "Q proofs" and forecast events actually happening, I was satisfied that the source, Q, whoever that might be, was legitimate.

As Editor/publisher of the international North Star Newsletter, which I had established in 2015, in mid-2018 I started researching many subjects referenced by Q and writing about them in my newsletter. I then dusted off my radio and television background as a newsreader and producer, and established a YouTube channel.

To date (May 2020) I have uploaded about 70 short videos. Collectively, they have had over a million views. The purpose was simply to condense many hours of investigative research into articles and videos that would be helpful to those who, for the most part, would be too busy to dig for themselves. After all, I was retired and had plenty of time to do the work. So all that resulted in writing and publishing my second book, *"Qanon And The Great Awakening,"* (https://amzn.to/37uOiVO) which has received some very good reviews.

Nevertheless, events keep unfolding, which brings us to this contribution. In early 2020 I came across what are known as The Toronto Protocols. There was a secret meeting in Toronto, Canada, in 1967 involving some very powerful individuals.

Their intention was to craft an agenda that would result in the take-over of America, which they deemed essential in their quest to literally control the world. You could perhaps see America as the "keystone" that would complete their arch of world control.

The journalist who eventually exposed them and wrote about their meeting in detail, "died of a heart attack" some years later, under very suspicious circumstances.

Suffice to say, there are some journalists who believe that the pen really is mightier than the sword. After missing the draft by a day, I volunteered to go to Vietnam as a war correspondent in the 1960s, so I suppose I am one of them – but, perhaps fortunately for me, the New Zealand Press Association canceled that gig at the last minute; they discovered it was cheaper to buy their stories from Reuters (which happens to have been controlled by the Illuminati for a century or more).

For some reporters and authors, the concept of the pen being mightier than the sword has, unfortunately, cost them their lives. Such was the case for the late Serge Monast, the French Canadian whose articles are referenced here because, in my mind, his death should not have been in vain.

Similarly, the late William (Bill) Cooper included in his book, *Behold a Pale Horse,* reference to secret weapons and silent wars – the war for your mind through mind control on many levels. Bill Cooper died in a shoot-out with the local sheriff and his deputies. Cooper killed one of the deputies before he was gunned down. The official story is that Cooper fired first.

There is another purpose here, and that relates to every reader; you in particular. In this book I am mentally taking you with me, to show you how to dig deep in your own voyage of discovery.

By doing our own research we become more enlightened, which means we are far better informed than those who are misinformed by today's Cabal media. We step outside the box of group-think that is deliberately perpetuated by the mainstream media and its propaganda narratives.

Then, sometimes with shock and dismay, we discover how much we have been lied to.

There is ample proof that the majority of today's media is no more than a tool of the Deep State. They are collectively referred to as the mainstream media, or MSM, but in my view, should be categorized as the DSM – Deep State Media. They have been active propagandists for a very long time.

Frankly, it was stomach-churning to find recently that Walter Cronkite, that CBS doyen of journalism, a man I admired for many years and even modeled my own role as a television reporter on back then, was in reality a front-man for the New World Order. I've even recently seen him recorded on film saying he stands by Satan! Well, R.I.P. Walter.
You will find little if any truth in the traditional media these days, for their propaganda role is to tell people what to think, not how to think. And this applies not only in America, but throughout the world.

What I have found is that we have been manipulated as a society, and as individuals, while the multiple facets of this New World Order agenda were quietly and gradually implemented.

As Q has said, this has happened by infiltration, rather than invasion – meaning, as we have seen with the upper echelons of the FBI, that many agencies have been infiltrated by Deep State supporters.

This has happened over the past five decades in particular, but even much further back than that as far as the world is concerned. My first book, *President Trump and the New World Order*, deals with that history.

This one deals with more current events. It includes reference to literally scores of original sources, with hyperlinks to the source where appropriate so you can do further research yourself. Naturally, they work with a click of a button in the ebook or Kindle version, but for the benefit of readers of the paperback they have been shortened (using bitly.com) to make it easier to type them into your search bar.

Now let's get on with exposing the Illuminati agenda, and shining a light on those dark places as we transition through the storm, into a better world.

- Michael Knight. May 2020

WHAT IS QANON?

Before we get to the Toronto Protocols, which were crafted in 1967 and updated in 1985, I believe we should start by giving them some present-day context, especially in regard to the Q movement.

To the uninformed it may seem outrageous that the Illuminati/Deep State (or Swamp) is being dealt with by Q, Q+ and a myriad Qanons; Q+ being understood to be President Trump using that signature on some of the more than 4000 posts that have been dropped since 2017.

There are many proofs of this among those posts at qanon.pub https://qanon.pub/? and on the primary Qanon research site – https://8kun.top/qresearch/index.html which anyone can check out or join anonymously.

Those who are known as Qanons, are as stated by General Michael Flynn, "an army of digital soldiers" who tirelessly research information in the Q posts on the Internet and share what they learn via social media. Much of this is done by way of memes - images overlaid with text, which according to Q cannot be identified or read by existing civilian technology.

Many of those memes feature a caricature of a frog. One must naturally wonder why, and why some memes and Q posts draw on scripture and refer to various books and verses from the Bible.

Try a search for Bible+frogs. A Bible dictionary will tell you:- "Frog (Heb. tsepharde'a, meaning a "marsh-leaper"). This reptile is mentioned in the Old Testament only in connection with one of the plagues which fell on the land of Egypt (Exodus 8:2-14; Psalms 78:45; 105:30)."

The frog caricature used by thousands of Qanons can therefore be seen to symbolize the "plague" that they are visiting upon the Illuminati.

Interestingly, Zuckerberg of Facebook has announced a $100,000 prize for anyone who can develop a way of identifying and reading such memes. The cover story is that Facebook wants to remove "hate speech" from its platform. What they really want to do is find and eliminate Qanon posts about subjects like Obamagate, Spygate, Fisagate and so forth.

As stated, those posts have seen hundreds of thousands of people beginning to "take the red pill" the red pill being a metaphor for waking up to the truth, as was illustrated in the movie The Matrix. Take the red pill and you open your eyes and your mind to what is really going on.

The blue pill? You stay the same, questioning nothing, in a cocoon of blissful ignorance.

Divided World

The whole world, not just America, is now divided precisely as the authors of the protocols intended. However, they never expected their schemes to come to light, and they never foresaw someone like President Trump being elected as president.

Nor did anyone at all expect Q and the Qanon movement to start the awakening process in 2017 that continues to ripple around the globe today.

Those who read Q's posts and do their own follow-up research are known as Qanons; "anon" of course is an abbreviation for "anonymous." While the vast majority of Qanons remain anonymous, thousands of them use avatars or pseudonyms on social media such as Twitter and YouTube, where many video channels, such as mine, now report on issues raised by those Q posts.

Some Qanons have become publicly known by name. One who is more well known than most is Jordan Sather. His definition of the Q movement is both concise and descriptive. He has written that Q is "An intelligence dissemination operation conducted by the White House and connected Military Intelligence insiders to BYPASS the Fake News Media and inform the public of an ongoing shadow civil war happening between Patriots and the Deep State."

On the other side of the Atlantic, Martin Geddes is a Londoner who has followed Q since the beginning. He now has over 150,000 followers on Twitter. That in itself tells us how the movement has mushroomed, especially when many of those followers themselves have thousands of followers.

Although we have not spoken or met in person, Martin's Q-related tweets and articles so impressed me that I asked him to contribute to what I now refer to as "our" book – *Qanon And The Great Awakening,*" (https://amzn.to/37uOiVO). His definition of Qanon, as of February 14 2020, comes in this tweet:- "The nature of the Q movement is the opposite of a cult. A cult is deceptive and coercive, telling you what to think, and having penalties for deviation from doctrine or apostasy. We are instead invited to exercise our critical thinking and free will, lending our voices willingly."

One of the memes or graphics to be found on the Internet, often on Twitter, says the following:-

"The Only Cult In History,
1. No-one has met the leader.
2. The leader insists you think for yourself.
3. Promotes non-violence and truth.
4. Our sole weapons are logic and research.
5. We pay no dues, we receive no pay nor glory.
"WWG1WGA (Where We Go One We Go All).
"Freedom is the Reward and Peace is the Prize."

Those descriptions are as good and accurate as you'll find anywhere. However, it is certainly not how the Fake News media portrays Q and the Qanons. And there's a reason for that, which has everything to do with their role as protectors of the Deep State itself, a fact which becomes painfully evident in the content of the Toronto Protocols.

Therein we find that the architects of the Globalists' plan had every intention of controlling the media in all its forms, thereby controlling what the public would be led to believe, and in essence, how to think.

That in itself should explain why today's legacy media has literally conspired (as in, a genuine conspiracy by definition) to portray Q and Qanons as a cult of the worst kind; a conspiracy theory of the far right whose adherents are nothing short of nut jobs.

Millions of Qanons

The truth is that one by one and little by little, the number of Qanons has grown from just a few individuals on a little-known message board in October 2017, to somewhere in the millions by early 2020.

Those numbers are clearly estimates, but they are not guesstimates. They are based on data which is understood to be related to the numbers of individual clicks on certain websites associated with the Q movement. So there are in fact millions of people throughout the world who are "waking up" and thereby thinking for themselves, assessing Q's posts, and discovering just how deep the swamp really is.

Since his first posts in October 2017, Q has followed with over 4000 additional "drops" as they're called.
For its part, the mainstream media has focused many negative articles on the Qanon movement, even going so far as to say it is a terrorist organization.
This is absolute nonsense.

Qanon has no formal structure. No headquarters. No single personality to be their "leader." Granted, there are many examples of individuals wearing T-shirts and clothing emblazoned with the letter Q, hundreds of them having been seen attending Trump rallies.

They and tens of thousands of others also wear the signature red "Make America Great Again" cap, and thousands of tweets use the abbreviation "MAGA." Another acronym is "WWG1WGA."

That got its start from its use by Q in various posts. It stems from the movie "White Squall" starring Jeff Bridges. As the skipper of a three-masted sailing ship crewed by an inexperienced group of young adults, he molds them into a team which must eventually work together when the vessel encounters a sudden massive storm known as a White Squall.
The team has become so united that the phrase "where we go one, we go all" (WWG1WGA) sums up the unity that has developed among them, and now Qanons.

SERGE MONAST – R.I.P.

Serge Monast was a French Canadian from Toronto; a poet, artist and investigative journalist.

Monast claimed there had been a secret meeting organized by the "6.6.6."

The numbers represented six individuals from each of three significant multinational enterprises.

They controlled the world's largest banks, energy resources, the agri-food industry, the international food trade, and what we now call Big Pharma.

Monast died suddenly in 1996 after being arrested (once again) and held in jail for 24 hours.

Just a few hours after his release he had a "heart attack." – which means to an experienced reporter such as myself (having seen many suspicious deaths reported over the years) that he was probably assassinated.

I like to think that his death was not in vain. His expose of the Toronto Protocols lives on.
The 1967 meeting, according to Monast, was about fine tuning their plans for world control.

Correctly and gradually implemented over a time span of several generations, it would eventually result in the imposition, or should we say acceptance, of a world government.

They planned to do that by ensuring their own control, behind the scenes, of economic, political and social policies.

THE TORONTO PROTOCOLS

The Toronto Protocols are just one small glimpse into the Illuminati's dark agenda.

They have been actively working toward their goal of a world government, under their control, for literally hundreds of years.

Much of that history is covered in my book, *President Trump and the New World Order,* since he is the man who stands between them and their final realization of world dominance.

When I first started learning about them, I was a naive believer in the good faith of our leaders. They might have their faults, since they were merely human, but to then begin to realize that some of them were capable of unimaginable atrocities was an absolute shock, to say the least.

There really is only one word that even comes close to defining them - Psychopath.

By definition, a psychopath is "a person who engages repeatedly in criminal and antisocial behavior without remorse or empathy for those victimized ... a pattern of lying, cunning, manipulating, exploiting, arrogance, delusions of grandeur."

Surely you'd have to be a psychopath to so callously plan so many ways to undermine society's traditional values, right down to seeing an infant as nothing more than a programmable asset. These psychopaths had been at their game long before their Toronto meeting.

In 1954 they held a meeting at Oosterbeek in the Netherlands. Now known as the Bilderbergers, they have been gathering annually ever since.

Participants at their 2014 60th anniversary meeting included "the heads of MI6, NATO, the International Monetary Fund, HSBC, Shell, BP and Goldman Sachs International, along with dozens of other chief executives, billionaires and high-ranking politicians from around Europe. This year also includes a visit from the supreme allied commander Europe, and a return of royalty – Queen Sofia of Spain and Princess Beatrix of the Netherlands, the daughter of the Bilderberg founder Prince Bernhard." (https://bit.ly/2Uklhra).

Now imagine a meme depicting a happy couple in 1950s attire smiling lovingly over their newborn child. It looks sweet, but the text is chilling. It reads:- "A woman with a newborn baby is too starry-eyed to see a rich man's cannon fodder or a cheap source of slave labor. A woman must, however, be conditioned to accept the transition to 'reality' when it occurs, or sooner. As the transition becomes more difficult to manage, the family unit must be carefully disintegrated, and state-controlled public education and state-operated child-care centers must become more common and legally enforced so as to begin the detachment of the child from the mother and father at an earlier age. (Mandatory) inoculation of behavioral drugs (Ritalin?) can speed the transition for the child."
Such is the mindset of these psychos.

Protocols in Brief

While you can read the full 1967 Toronto Protocols document at this link (https://bit.ly/35PmAmJ) for the sake of brevity I will simply paraphrase what Monast said was stated in the record of that meeting of the 6.6.6.

They talked about creating multinational companies, establishing Humanitarian and Food Aid projects internationally, the purpose being to siphon off the billions of dollars involved in such programs to finance their own endeavors.

They talked about genocide, but not only by way of wars and revolutions such as their forebears had instigated to bring Communism to power in Russia and China. Genocide could be achieved in much subtler ways. For instance, advancing the use of chemicals that could result in cancer at some time well past their initial use. That in turn would lead to a multi-billion-dollar windfall for those engaged in cancer research and treatment, so long as no cure would be made public.

Perhaps their master stroke was their understanding of how easily people at all levels of society can be controlled through their emotions and desires; if you can manipulate these in an individual, you can use the same strategy on an entire society, a nation, and the world.

Central to that strategy would be control of the media, which in turn would be used to promote a range of emotionally charged narratives and subjects. Seemingly benign on the face of it, the underlying intent would be to mold society's thinking as individuals and as a collective in ways that would benefit the goals of the Illuminati.

Noting what they called "the errancy of men," the 6.6.6. planned to promote a variety of themes that would effectively result in the dissolution of the family unit, the embrace of deviant behaviors, schisms between races and ethnic groups, a dependency on government, and eventually an unquestioning demand for the imposition of a system of global governance.

Infiltration of the media, the use of Hollywood films and its many deviant themes would all be used to mold public thinking along carefully predetermined lines.

The result has been evident in western society for some time. Conditioned to thinking of self interest first, we have become a society in which sex, drugs, sports, and leisure activities are our preferred antidotes to the fears associated with the struggle for economic survival.

Our emotions drive our perceptions and decisions; we almost blindly accept the media's brainwashing and daily propaganda, effectively allowing others to do our thinking for us.

Infiltration

The Illuminati are the polar opposite. They are powerful but secretive individuals, who, according to one of the Rockefellers on record in a taped interview, see it as their responsibility to look after their own families.

Perhaps that seems like a laudable thing, except that to do so, they are prepared to manipulate everyone they deem to be below their station in order to create the world according to their image.

They have embedded their "disciples" (for want of a better term) in the fields of politics, education, law, finance, child welfare services, religion, industry, governments and government agencies, the military, the United Nations and its subsidiaries; and this infiltration has occurred not only in America, but throughout the world.

A major point from those Toronto Protocols is that they deemed it vital to undermine and eventually eliminate the juedo-Christian ethic that was the foundation of the traditional family unit. Cunningly, to say the least, they successfully promoted "child protection services" and agencies. So successful has that been that today, it's almost as if the "rights of the child" take precedence over the rights of the parents.

A simple Internet search on "child protection services" will yield results showing that such "services" have been established world-wide. Just one example (https://bit.ly/2Wa9cGs):-
"Child protection Minnesota has various programs to help children who may not be in safe environments. County and tribal child protection workers work with families to prevent child maltreatment or, in some cases, work with the courts and law enforcement to remove children from the home if they are in harm's way."

What the 6.6.6. participants wanted was to create a future world in which children would have no respect for their parents, and would in fact be prepared to rat on them (for some real or imagined event) as did the children of the Soviet Union in the 1950s.

The United Nations has since implemented much of this protocol via their conventions "on the rights of the child." (https://bit.ly/2A9aUzh).

The use of rock groups, film stars and singers like Madonna and Lady Gaga has advanced the goal of corrupting if not completely eliminating the morals of many of today's young people - not to mention those who are now adults with their own dysfunctional families.

Programmed by an education system that no longer teaches the truths of history, and lacking any concept of family values, too many of them believe that "freedom" and "individuality" means there are no boundaries to self indulgence. Many, like the Hitler Youth of days gone by, now embrace the anarchic mantras of groups such as Antifa and Black Lives Matter. . Others, regrettably, are lost in a whirlwind of drugs and indiscriminate sex and the resultant depression, self hatred, and eventual suicide.

Saying anything about women these days is fraught with its own perils. But they too have been targeted deliberately as part of this plan to totally disrupt the family, the community, and society at large.

There should be no discounting the fact that the introduction of the birth control pill was in many ways a tremendous benefit to millions of women. It allowed them and their considerate "other" (a male, no less) to consciously determine their own family planning while enjoying marital bliss, so to speak, without the underlying fear that this just might result in yet another mouth to feed.

Dominated for far too long by men in general, women could now do what men have always done – play around in this new age of sexual liberation. (If I recall correctly, that was a very good thing for us men too.)

The downside to the introduction of the pill, correctly foreseen by those who had it introduced in the first place, was an increase in divorce and abortions, once again playing into that scenario of gradually destroying the family unit and its judeo-Christian underpinnings.
In addition, this era of burgeoning sexual liberation saw girls at ever younger ages becoming sexually active, often pregnant, suffering the very real pangs of remorse and whatever despair goes with having an abortion. Subsequently, many, including the young males involved, would become drug addicts, alcoholics, and/or suicidal.

What one gains from a careful reading and analysis of the Protocols can be boiled down to a number of salient bullet points. I call it a bucket list.

6.6.6. BUCKET LIST

Whoever those 18 individuals were who met in Toronto in 1967, and whoever leaked the information to Serge Monast, his detailed article can be reduced to a list of things that the 6.6.6. planned to do to take over the world, especially America.

Following is my condensed version and understanding of what I believe to have been the 38 main action points of their plan. Later chapters will deal with some of them in detail.

- Infiltrate politics, the legal system and education.
- Abolish morality
- Break up the family.
- Create then remove the middle class.
- Hide intent behind the illusion of Democracy.
- Organize and infiltrate student protests.
- Separate children from parents.
- Wipe out parental authority.
- Encourage children to report parents.
- Produce a Soviet-like society (socialism).
- Eliminate judeo-Christian instruction.
- Promote equality of all religions, cults, sorcery and magic.
- Utilize the power of the United Nations.
- Introduce "Child Protection Services," and "The Rights of the Child."

- Cause the collapse and fall of nations.
- Discontinue teaching religion, history, good manners.
- Dilute mathematics and language.
- Create arrogant, contemptuous, delinquent youth.
- Disrupt traditional care of the elderly.
- Give precedence to the "Rights of the Individual" over the rights of the majority.
- Encourage sexual freedom to the point of obsession, which has always collapsed societies – such as Rome.
- Use chemistry (The Pill?) to relegate moral principles to oblivion.
- Infiltrate all women's movements to ensure final breakdown of family.
- Use sexual liberation to collapse prior moral and religious constraints.
- Normalize sexual liberty.
- Divide people against each other.
- Push youth toward damaging experiences, e.g. early sexuality.
- Push alcohol and drugs which lead to suicide.
- Make divorce and abortion socially acceptable.
- Control the economies of Nation States (and thereby their people).
- Eventually cut off all means of survival for the Middle Class.
- Bloat agencies with career public servants, thus a "government within the government" to be used regardless of which party is in power.
- Buy (or *eliminate*) CEOs, state agency heads, and those "whose work and efficiency might give too much power to the Nation-States." (T*he 2016 death under very suspicious circumstances of Associate Justice of the*

Supreme Court, Antonin Scalia comes to mind. (https://bit.ly/2L9a3Ro)

- Control all media information.
- Depopulate rural areas. Overpopulate cities. Eliminates independence.
- Create agricultural cooperatives – and infiltrate them.
- Use the State (controlled politicians) to sow divisions between diverse cultures by stressing "rights of minorities" over "national unity."
- Then "use the UN to impose our New World Order."

CONSPIRACY THEORIES

The term "Conspiracy Theory" was invented by the CIA in order to prevent disbelief of official government stories.

It was coined by agents of the elite to counter such truth as is uncovered and revealed by those who question the official and media propaganda narrative.

The truth is that the thrust toward a New World Order is in fact the real conspiracy. It is a genuine conspiracy by the elite, dating back long before the Toronto Protocols were enumerated.

That gathering of 18 individuals (the 6.6.6.) was simply intended to fine tune their conspiracy. They met in secret to discuss their seditious intentions, and that is the true definition of a conspiracy; individuals or a group who conspire together to achieve a certain outcome.

Another genuine conspiracy, which is also under their control, can be seen in the mainstream media and its coordinated Trump-hating articles.

For over four years now, the Democrats, with full support of much of the media, has regaled America with the "Russia Russia Russia" refrain, keeping millions of minds focused on that subject with all their associated lies and spurious claims.

They know that if you tell a lie often enough, it becomes an accepted "truth" in the mind of the recipient. It is especially effective when presented by those who are assumed to have authority, such as politicians and the people who front the hundreds of media outlets around America, and the world.

Maxine Waters and other Democrats, such as House Speaker Nancy (Ice Cream) Pelosi use this ploy by constantly berating President Trump, saying Democrats will be relentless in investigating him even if acquitted of impeachment charges by the Senate, as he was, unanimously.

Waters insists that she knows of a "secret deal" between Putin and Trump (though she has no proof); that "Trump needs to be imprisoned and placed in solitary confinement;" and that Trump is "an illegitimate racist occupying the White House." (https://bit.ly/35EpU3T).
Obviously it works, but in several ways, one being that this ploy is counterproductive. While n the one hand it ensures continued votes from those who agree with such madness, on the other, it fuels the "walkaway" movement by those who are leaving the Democrat party.

These people think independently, seeing the vast difference between the foisted narrative and what the president actually says and does. For his supporters, and those becoming disenchanted with the endless Democrat falsehoods, the president is admired for "promises made, promises kept."

Yet perhaps most importantly from the point of view of those whose own closets are full of skeletons, and who have signed onto the New World Order agenda, such protestations and endless investigations only work to delay the inevitable disclosure of their own corruption, which in some cases has even had the president use the term "treason."

He certainly said that about Adam Schiff – who fortunately for himself is protected by the fact that he can say what he likes, be it lies or truth (and always lies about the president) within the protected halls of Congress.

That's why Schiff could say, without batting an eye, and time after time, that there was "indisputable proof" that the president had colluded with Russia. And then along came the Ukraine issue, with Schiff and cronies echoing the same old charges, going so far as to present articles of impeachment to the Senate, and losing yet another battle in their drive to remove the president before he reveals to the public what he has found out about them.

Schiff and others in Congress who constantly denigrate the president, and in Schiff's case use blatant fabrications, know very well that they are protected by the Constitution itself – although with one particular exception that could well come home to roost.

Article 1 Section 6 of the Constitution states:- "They [Congress] shall in all Cases, except Treason, Felony and Breach of the Peace, be privileged from Arrest during their Attendance at the Session of their respective Houses, and in going to and returning from the same; and for any Speech or Debate in either House, they shall not be questioned in any other Place" (https://bit.ly/2WuyeQF).

The exception that just might see Schiff's undoing is stated in just one word – Treason.

REAL FAKE NEWS

As for the self-destructing mainstream media, as a lifelong Old School ethical journalist myself, I can say unequivocally that today's mainstream media no longer serves the public.

Instead, as you will see, it has been co-opted and impregnated with individuals whose job is to protect the guilty and control the public narrative. That simply means their job is to tell people what to think, not how to think.

In short, they want people in the United States to think that President Trump is totally unfit for the job, and they miss no opportunity to beat that drum. As well, it is obvious to them and their controllers that the information being posted by Q, then researched by Qanons, then posted and retweeted thousands of times, is progressively revealing the depth of corruption, not to mention satanic activity, within the ranks of the Deep State. That is why the mainstream media, owned, literally, by globalist corporations, has abandoned any pretense at honest journalism.

Q frequently says "think logically." In that case, does not logic make it clear that journalists in the legacy media have as much access to the Q drops and Qanon research as anyone else? Of course they do.

If they were honest, they would by now have asked the president himself, "Who is Q?" But no, for two years and counting they have avoided that question. What might be the logical answer as to why?

Given that logic and reason should go hand in hand, the only reason I can think of, again as a career journalist, is that they are no longer journalists. They are nothing more than Deep State propaganda purveyors. Ironically, they may know nothing at all themselves about the Illuminati, but many of them have CIA and intelligence community roots.

That can be deduced from the fact that CNN's Anderson Cooper, for just one example, is known to have been a CIA intern before he became a "journalist." And in the decades that I personally worked in all branches of the media, I certainly met a few individuals with intelligence agency credentials.

However, to be as fair as possible, it's probable that most reporters are simply doing a job, which means doing as they're told by their immediate superiors, who in turn do what they're told by their superiors. It is the owners, the board and the presidents of these companies who set the rules, so even if there are reasonably ethical reporters on staff, they know full well that they have to toe the line.

Long before he decided to run for the presidency, Donald Trump became accustomed to media coverage, both good and bad. Even so, it is remarkable how firmly he handles the press since he gained the White House. To roars of approval he'll call them "Fake News" at every rally, and rightly so, because the facts speak for themselves; the media makes up stories, makes up "sources" and does its utmost to make the president look bad.

These days, ninety percent of the mainstream media is a propaganda machine. It cannot be trusted. And yet for decades, it has been used as a brainwashing or mind control asset of the Illuminati, exactly as they planned so long ago in Toronto.

PROJECT MOCKINGBIRD

Why is most of the mainstream media untrustworthy? Because it is a modern-day propaganda machine.

It is on record that the CIA planted as many as 400 of their trained "journalists" in the media under a project known as Operation Mockingbird by some, or Project Mockingbird by others.

Quoting from a CIA document released to theblackvault.com (https://bit.ly/2Wc2iAx) and for some reason titled "Family Jewels," we find that the CIA was also spying on journalists in Washington DC back in the 1960s.

The relevant paragraph reads "Project Mockingbird – During the period from 12 March 1963 to 15 June 1963, this office installed telephone taps on two Washington-based newsmen who were suspected of disclosing classified information obtained from a variety of governmental sources."

However, those documents do not mention anything about inserting "newsmen" into the media.

Turning to Wikipedia, but aware that it can be altered at any time, we find that "A wide range of CIA operations were examined in a series of Congressional investigations from 1975 to 1976 including CIA ties with journalists.

The most extensive discussion of CIA relations with news

media from these investigations is in the Church Committee's Final Report, published in April 1976. The report covered CIA ties with both foreign and domestic news media.

Wikipedia says "For foreign news media, the report concluded that:- "The CIA currently maintains a network of several hundred foreign individuals around the world who provide intelligence for the CIA and at times attempt to influence opinion through the use of covert propaganda." These individuals provide the CIA with direct access to a large number of newspapers and periodicals, scores of press services and news agencies, radio and television stations, commercial book publishers, and other foreign media outlets.

"For domestic media, the report states:- "Approximately 50 of the [Agency] assets are individual American journalists or employees of US. media organizations. Of these, fewer than half are 'accredited' by US. media organizations …. The remaining individuals are non-accredited freelance contributors and media representatives abroad … More than a dozen United States news organizations and commercial publishing houses formerly provided cover for CIA agents abroad. A few of these organizations were unaware that they provided this cover."

It's up to you as to whether or not you believe the CIA's response, which was that:- "Prior to the release of the Church report, the CIA had already begun restricting its use of journalists.

According to the report, former CIA director William Colby informed the committee that in 1973 he had issued instructions that 'As a general policy, the Agency will not make any clandestine use of staff employees of US. publications which have a substantial impact or influence on public opinion.'"

"In February 1976, Director George H. W. Bush announced an even more restrictive policy: 'effective immediately, CIA will not enter into any paid or contractual relationship with any full-time or part-time news correspondent accredited by any US. news service, newspaper, periodical, radio or television network or station.'"

"By the time the Church Committee Report was completed, all CIA contacts with accredited journalists had been dropped. The Committee noted, however, that 'accredited correspondent' meant the ban was limited to individuals 'formally authorized by contract or issuance of press credentials to represent themselves as correspondents' and that non-contract workers who did not receive press credentials, such as stringers or freelancers, were not included.

"Journalist Carl Bernstein, writing in an October 1977 article in the magazine Rolling Stone, claims that the Church Committee report 'covered up' CIA relations with news media, and names a number of journalists whom he says worked with the CIA."

What's missing from Wikipedia's review of the Church Committee's hearings is any mention of Project or Operation Mockingbird. Perhaps it's missing by design?
However, what is included are the words of Senator Frank Church himself, when in 1975 he appeared on NBC's Meet The Press, and "discussed the NSA without naming them."

Speaking of the technology available to the NSA in the 1970s, he said "that capability at any time could be turned around on the American people, and no American would have any privacy left: such is the capability to monitor everything – telephone conversations, telegrams, it doesn't matter. There would be no place to hide" (and) "the most careful effort to combine together in resistance to the government, no matter how privately it was done, is within the reach of the government to know. Such is the capability of this technology."

It was that very technology, and the advent of computers, that the crafters of the Toronto Protocols intended to utilize not just in America, but on a global scale.

GOOD UNMASKING BAD

Frankly, I find it quite amazing that the NSA has had those surveillance capabilities for so many decades.

Back then, the CIA was also physically and illegally opening snail mail, rather than simply taking note of who the letters were addressed to and from.
What is clear now, is that the NSA, the CIA, the FBI and the DOJ have been tools of the Globalists from their very inception.

They have controlled the public narrative with considerable ease, simply because we were brought up to believe that those in authority were tellers of truth and guardians of us and our rights.

Government agencies and their personnel were there to make sure we abided by the rules, but at the same time, their job at least in the justice-related departments, was to keep us safe from harm. Politicians, foundations, charities, aid programs and the Red Cross were all (so I thought then) working for the common good.

What we (or should I say I) had not realized nor understood was that hidden within all the good words and allegedly good works was insidious duplicity. It is truly disturbing to discover that "good" has been used by these controllers for decades, if not centuries, as a cover for everything they do that is beyond bad. It is pure evil.

As Director of the CIA George H.W. Bush stated there would be no further use of CIA journalist/assets. As a public relations move that certainly sounded like the truth. However, as the later report noted, he had left the way open to continue that very activity, but in a different manner. The CIA would continue to use freelancers and contract reporters to feed the media.

It is nothing short of embarrassing to realize we have been deliberately fooled for so long.

On the other hand, there's a great sense of relief when you discover the truth. Unfortunately, some of it can be extremely hard to believe when it starts to expose the evil deeds of so many among those we have voted into office, who have betrayed both us and the values we hold dear.

Perhaps a greater peace of mind is achieved by knowing that this is finally being dealt with – once and for all.

Russia! Russia! Russia!

Nowadays, all this US media talk echoing the Democrats' "Russia! Russia! Russia!" narrative, is a deliberate smoke screen to prevent people from paying any attention to what previous administrations and leading politicians have gotten away with, and also allowed China to get away with.

We'll come back to that, but for now let us dig into this fixation on the lie about Trump and Russia.

By way of background, statistics compiled by impartial observers have shown that mainstream media coverage of President Trump has been something like 95% negative ever since he announced he would run for the presidency, and that was four years ago.

How many thousands of articles, radio shows, television news broadcasts and talk shows does that entail? Literally thousands of hours, all intended to control what people think by telling them what to think.

Oddly enough, while the president is the recipient of the most negative coverage in the nation, Q has pointed out that Qanons come in a close second. Independent sources have shown that to be the case.

The obvious question is, why?

Perhaps we can find a logical answer in an excerpt from Q's Post 2682 of February 10 2019.

He said "define projection," referring to a news article published that day by The Hill under the headline, "The case for Russia collusion … against the Democrats." (https://bit.ly/3bdDsof).

It was written by John Solomon, one of the few remaining journalists worthy of respect for their "old school" approach to the craft.

Solomon's first two paragraphs:- "With Republicans on both House and Senate investigative committees having found no evidence of Donald Trump being guilty of Democrat-inspired allegations of Russian collusion, it is worth revisiting one anecdote that escaped significant attention during the hysteria but continues to have US security implications.

"As secretary of State, Hillary Clinton worked with Russian leaders, including Foreign Minister Sergey Lavrov and then-President Dmitri Medvedev, to create US technology partnerships with Moscow's version of Silicon Valley, a sprawling high-tech campus known as Skolkovo."

He adds that *"The collaboration occurred at the exact same time Bill Clinton made his now infamous trip to Russia to pick up a jaw-dropping $500,000 check for a single speech."*

In referencing that article, Q's post was unusually lengthy, and if this is the first time you've seen a Q post, you'll find that it also seems rather cryptic, presenting statements in the form of questions, and using single letters in some cases (as in D for Democrats).

One reason for this Socratic format, which is to start a debate with a question, is that in Q's case, the method avoids directly making statements that could be construed as harming national security or breaching some form of high level security clearance.

The objective is to encourage readers to think, think, think – pause and think – and follow through with personal research. It is this personal involvement that has seen countless individuals reject the propaganda narrative as they find for themselves, thanks to Q's questions, how far from the truth the official narrative has strayed.

Q's post goes on to say:-
"Define 'Projection'.
"How do you fix something that is known to be broken (corrupt)? "Do you first need to remove those responsible? "Think FBI/DOJ 'exit' list. "How do you 'restore' the image (public faith) of our most prestigious 'law enforcement' institutions? "Hold people accountable? "Equal justice under the law?
"The battle begins (as seen today) w/ public opinion.
"The FIGHT to win PUBLIC FAVORABILITY.
"The FIGHT to control the NARRATIVE.
"How do D's control the NARRATIVE?
"1) FAKE NEWS MEDIA push of 'by design' narrative [daily updates – 4am] (Ed Note – talking points and buzz words are dis-

tributed 4am daily to all Deep State-controlled media outlets.)
"2) FAKEWOOD echo of 'by design' narrative (Ed Note – Hollywood.)
"3) SOCIAL MEDIA stream/promote of 'by design' narrative + censor/block/ban of challenger(s) of that narrative
"Do they provide evidence to support their conclusions?
"POTUS/RUSSIA narrative – evidence?
"None.
"POTUS racist narrative - evidence?
"None.
"POTUS ....(you can play this game all day long)
"'None'.
"What do they count on?
"How many experiments have been conducted by the C_A re: mind control?
"Psych 101: If you hear & see something over and over again by multiple (supposedly credible) news agencies, elected officials, actors/actresses, documentaries on TV, movies, internet, social media, foreign press etc. all pushing the same narrative/conclusions.......what happens?
"Do FACT-LESS claims become FACTS in the minds of many?
"Do they count on the fact that w/ work, family, stresses of life, etc. that the typical person does not have enough time in the day to research topics for themselves and therefore would believe narratives projected in the echo chamber w/o the need to provide facts or substance other than opinion?
"Why do they try so hard to keep you DIVIDED by race, gender, class, ...?
"Notice an increase in this push over the past 2-years?
"Are you stronger together/UNITED or DIVIDED?
"If you dare to challenge their narrative are you cast out [banned] by society as a threat/conspiracy theorist etc..?
"Are you cast out by members of your own family?
"'DIVIDED'
"'Group-Think'
"THEY DO NOT WANT YOU TO THINK FOR YOURSELF.

"A FREE-THINKING 'LOGICAL' PERSON WHO DRAWS CONCLUSIONS BASED ON FACTS ARE, PUT SIMPLY, A THREAT TO THEIR CONTROL/POWER GRIP.
"ALL THEY CARE ABOUT IS CONTROL [I.E. POWER].
"WITH CONTROL COMES PERSONAL GAIN.
"They want to keep you poor and in need of government assistance.
"Bigger the gov't, the more CONTROL they have, the more POWER they possess.
"When you are in need, you are weak.
"When you are weak, you are not strong.
"When you are not strong, you do not FIGHT BACK.
"This is as real as it gets.
"They never thought she would lose.
"Why? See above re: Control.
"Transparency is the only way forward.
"Transparency is the only way to PROVE TO THE PUBLIC that everything SOLD TO YOU as TRUTH was nothing but a FAKE NARRATIVE DESIGNED TO KEEP, YOU, THE PEOPLE, POWERLESS, AND KEEP THEM, IN CONTROL [I.E. IN POWER].
"FAKE NEWS' [propaganda arm of the Democrat machine] sole responsibility is to prevent the TRUTH from ever being disseminated to the masses.
"Mass Infiltration (everywhere).
"Transparency is the only way forward re: public opinion.
"Prosecution is the only way forward re: save & defend the rule of law.
"Prosecution and Transparency is the only way to save our way of life.
"Q."

The Illuminati have had their puppets – whether willing or blackmailed but puppets nevertheless – elected many times in the United States, but the very fact that this country was founded as a Republic, with a Constitution and Bill of Rights, including the right to bear arms, required that as far as this nation was concerned, they would have to gradually infiltrate the halls of power, and oh so gradually achieve their goals.

China! China! China!

We don't have to look back too far to see how successful the "6.6.6." were in having their protocols surreptitiously implemented.

Using their Judas goats in the American government, the Illuminati have fooled a nation of sheep into accepting many of their schemes.

Their strategy has been nearly flawless, for they have used their corrupt political adherents to enact laws and create deals that at first glance appear to be for the benefit of the nation. In reality many such laws further the Globalists' agenda while lining the pockets of their proponents.

While the Toronto Protocols do not mention any country by name, it is logical to assume that their goal of a New World Order would require control of every country on the planet, China included.

They managed to turn Russia into a communist nation, and no doubt they had a hand in China's Communist revolution under Mao Tse-tung, aka Mao Zedong. In Russia, under Stalin, some 30 million people were eliminated.

In China, under Mao and the succeeding Chinese Communist Party, many millions more have lost their lives.\ Aside from those cold-blooded depopulation pogroms, China would prove to be a very useful pawn in their efforts to take control of the United States.

This would not necessarily be by way of an all-out traditional war, though that fear would continuously play a part in conditioning people to believe that peace can only be achieved by establishing a world government.

Instead of war, China has been very successful in what can be termed a "silent war."

Through multiple agreements made by past administrations, China has become an indispensable trading partner for America. Yet while America has relied on cheap products from China for decades, US factories have closed by the score.

Then President Trump came along and quickly moved to change the balance of trade, bring manufacturing back home, and rewrite those trade agreements that favored China at America's expense.

Commerce can therefore be seen as one ingredient in that silent war. Another is China's proven ability to find, target and work with corruptible American politicians at many levels.

One of the big payoffs for China was the Long Beach port agreement.

China's Long Beach "Invasion"

Invasions don't have to all be like those conducted using military might and extreme force with all the loss of life that involves.

Invasions can be the exact opposite – silent, effective, yet in the long run, perhaps even more effective than a full-on assault which only leaves behind a ruined landscape and years of reconstruction.

Instead, a silent invasion in the terms presented here, would be an invasion using commerce as the front, trade as a useful weapon, and mutual agreements or business partnerships between apparently peace-preserving individuals on both sides.

Q has dropped many posts about such issues. Personal research leads to the inescapable conclusion that the previous administration, and even those going back many many years, with few exceptions were the silent vehicles for moving ahead with the imposition of the New World Order.

That's why in 2012 Obama and the State Department and whoever else should have been responsible for looking after America's national security, had no problem with allowing a Chinese communist company to sign a 40-year lease for the Long Beach Port facility. But we're getting ahead of ourselves.

Clinton Backs China

Background:- As I researched this issue, I recalled something about Bill Clinton allowing China to lease and control a massive port terminal in Los Angeles. I first learned about it shortly after I moved to America in 1990, and wondered at the time why on earth would the United States give an avowed enemy access to a major port facility?

It honestly didn't make sense at the time. But knowing what I know now, it underscores what I have learned from the Protocols. To refresh my memory and get some facts, I did a search for "Clinton China."Among the results was an americanthink.com article about China having a "Most Favored Nation" status (https://bit.ly/2zfjSuv).

When it comes to Communist China, which for decades has been portrayed as an enemy of the United States, I was surprised to learn that in 1993 President Bill Clinton signed Executive Order 12850 (https://bit.ly/2WasTOc). It was that which started a process that would see literally thousands of jobs lost in America as the Globalist overlords of industry closed factory after factory.

It also saw the US-China trade deficit balloon from $18 billion in 1993, to $367 billion in 2015.

Incidentally, in June that year Donald Trump announced he intended to run for office. With its Most Favored Nation status, China only had to pay 6% in tariffs, instead of the 40% which otherwise would have been required. Was he aware of how well China had benefited from that deal?

What Clinton's EO did was to wrest from Congress the annual review of China's "Most Favored Nation" status by arbitrarily transferring that responsibility to the State Department, which in turn is headed by a secretary appointed by the president.

That, says the article, "established a Democratic strategy for manipulating foreign policy that was copied by both Hillary while she was Secretary of State and Obama while he was president."
Now about that port facility in California.
Just three years after signing that Executive Order, in 1996 Clinton allowed China to sign a long lease of a 145-acre former Navy base in Long Beach California, Long Beach at that time being where up to a quarter of all imports from China reached the United States.

Significantly, the China Ocean Shipping Company (Cosco), is owned by China's communist government, but, more interesting still, the lease was signed just three weeks after one of the company's ships was raided and found to be carrying "several thousand automatic weapons that Federal officials say were headed for Los Angeles street gangs."(https://nyti.ms/3bbE0e7).

What in hindsight could be interpreted as a turning of the blind eye to that event is the fact that California Senators Feinstein and Boxer called for the White House to investigate, asking if there were any reasons not to allow the lease.

The "Inquiry" Scam

What happened was straight out of what you could call the politicians' playbook, because it is a ploy that has been used by governments around the world for a very long time. It goes like this. Something happens that raises questions, sometimes very legitimate questions, in the public's mind. One or more politicians then appear to take the public's questions seriously, and they call for an inquiry.

The government sets up an inquiry, usually headed by someone appointed by the government, and before long, a report is produced. It placates the vast majority of the public, and the government carries on with whatever scheme or plan they had to advance their New World Order objective.

They are of course assisted by the mainstream media, which may initially ask a few softball questions, or pretend (fake) concern, but eventually they move on to some other topic to divert public attention.

In the case of those thousands of firearms being found on an incoming Chinese ship, and the call by Feinstein and Boxer for an investigation, nothing happened. There was no inquiry. In fact, an unnamed Pentagon official is quoted as having said "We are not aware of any reason for concern," and the deal went ahead.

China got yet another foothold in America.

Senator Feinstein, by the way, had employed a Chinese-American man for 20 years who turned out to be a spy for China.

He doubled as an office staffer and as her driver until being caught by the FBI in 2013. (https://bit.ly/3cpt12l). Dianne Feinstein and her husband have had a very close relationship with the communist Chinese for decades, as per this in-depth report (https://bit.ly/2A990P9) in The Federalist. It has been worth many millions of dollars.

Cosco, (not to be confused with the US company, Costco) therefore got control of one of America's biggest port facilities with the blessing of Clinton, and later, Obama as well.

In July 2017, six months after President Trump's inauguration, the Chinese government (that is, in the form of Cosco) solidified its control of the port by purchasing a controlling share of another Chinese shipping company, Orient Overseas Container Line (OOCL), one of the largest shipping enterprises in the world.

OOCL and the Port authority – with the blessing of Obama's administration – had met in Hong Kong in 2012 to sign an agreement giving OOCL a 40-year container terminal lease. (https://bit.ly/2L5sl69). This, no doubt, was a major incentive for Cosco to spend $6.3 billion to gain a controlling 75 per cent holding in OOCL.

Because of the millions it would be putting into upgrading the port, OOCL was much loved by the Port of Long Beach which was moving ahead with its Middle Harbor Redevelopment Project.

Imagine – a 40-year lease on a major port facility on the West Coast of America.

Think about this. As stated, Cosco got its initial lease at Long Beach despite the fact that one of its ships had been attempting to smuggle thousands of automatic weapons into America. It is all but certain that those weapons would have been found in containers on that ship. Containers are a modern-day smuggler's best friend. Here's why.

Container ship capacity is measured in TEU (Twenty Foot Equivalent Units) which refers to one 20ft long container. The largest container ship in the world is the OOCL Hong Kong. It can carry 21,413 20ft containers.
Allowing 5280ft per mile, that's 264 containers per mile – or, in total, those 21,413 containers laid end to end would form a line 81 miles long. And that's not including the trucks carrying them.

Why is that significant?

Because it is clearly impossible for any customs or other inspection agency to check every single incoming container; and because shipping containers are the perfect way to carry contraband, be it weapons, or drugs, or people ensnared in the global human trafficking trade.

How To Get Rich

This odd relationship between the United States and China at both the commerce and political levels goes back a long way.

This is clearly evident in the relationship that former Vice President Joe Biden and his son Hunter created with China. It was a relationship that netted Hunter Biden an interest in a deal worth $1.5 billion.

This has not escaped the notice of President Trump and Q.
In Post 3381 of July 8 2019, Q says:-
Joe Biden (Vice President of the United States)
Follow the Family
Corruption in DC > How to Get Rich
Are Liberals willfully blind or ……….?
(https://washex.am/3fwghZm).

Biden's brother $1.5b contract in Iraq. (https://bit.ly/3cjBKTG).
Biden's son $1.5b deal w/ China.
Coincidence?
DRAIN THE SWAMP.
Q

I promise to use this play on words only once, so here goes... the 40-year lease deal has been "Trumped."

A Wall Street Journal story (https://bit.ly/2YHiDPl) of May 8 2019 explains how that deal was dismantled.

Cosco was told by the Trump administration that it had to sell its controlling share, which it did, to an Australian company. It still stands to make more than a billion dollars one way or another, but its 40-year lease has been nullified.

The WSJ says in closing:- "This decision to slap China on the wrist seems to confirm that the Trump administration is serious about holding the feet of America's rival to the fire, and the president was not making empty promises on the campaign trail when he promised to put America first in international deals."

SPIES FOR CHINA

If a United States person, or one who is legally in the United States, also has a close relationship with Communist China, is such a person really a spy, or a traitor, or just a useful individual whose work in America can be legally transferred to Communist China?

If the Globalists intended to undermine this country, which they assuredly did, could they have used their assets in US politics to create legal ways in which to circumvent any suggestion of spying while at the same time allowing Communist China to purloin a treasure trove of information that text book spies might have once risked their lives for?

Think about that as we proceed.

Communist China is well known for ripping off American patents, intellectual property, and technology. It has also sent thousands of its young people to be educated in American colleges and universities. It has donated many millions of dollars to US universities, by way of grants to professors and researchers in many disciplines of interest to Communist China. Beyond that, many more millions, probably even billions have gone into buying land and property and businesses.

Communist China has done the same in many other countries, from Australia (it is said to own something like 25 per cent of the land there) to Africa, the Middle East and Europe, Italy being a particular beneficiary.

This has not gone unnoticed by the Trump administration.

An associate professor at the University of Tennessee, Knoxville, was arrested February 28 2020 and charged with wire fraud and lying about his relationship with China.(https://bit.ly/3cduqsz).

He worked in the Department of Mechanical, Aerospace and Biomedical Engineering, any advances in which would be of great interest to the Chinese government.
His name, Anming Hu.

What is notable about his and other arrests is that there has been a country-wide crackdown on China's influence on the American education system only since President Trump took office.

Prior to that, to put it in the bluntest and most factual terms, America was for sale. It was being sold out by corrupt individuals for personal gain. Most notable in that regard would be the fact that then vice president Joe Biden took his son to China, and right after they left, Hunter Biden scored a seat on a board involved in something like a $1.5 billion venture.

Hillary's Emails

Although at the time of this writing it had yet to be fully revealed to the public, while she was Secretary of State, Hillary Clinton used a private email server for top secret emails.

Q has noted that China was in the loop. That means China was literally receiving copies of all the emails transmitted through that *insecure* system, including those that were marked Classified or Top Secret.

This is Q's take on that, from Post 3045 of March 13 2019. It starts with a link to a Tweet by Rep John Ratcliffe on March 12 2019, and just in case it has been censored by now, it reads:- "Lisa Page confirmed to me under oath that the FBI was ordered by the Obama DOJ not to consider charging Hillary Clinton for gross negligence in the handling of classified information." (https://bit.ly/2A0MHei).

Q then references "the tarmac meeting" which was between Bill Clinton and then Attorney General Loretta Lynch, during which, according to Q, Lynch was offered a Supreme Court nomination under the expected Hillary Clinton presidency, provided she quashed the investigation into Hillary Clinton's use of an insecure server.

Says Q:-
Days Later....
[JC] (*That's James Comey*) "No charges are appropriate.........."
HOW DID HRC OBTAIN SAP (Special Access Programs) ON HER PERSONAL SERVER(S)?
ACCESS TO SAP/SCI IS RECORDED IN A LOCAL ACCESS REGISTER OR IN A COMPUTER DATABASE --- WHERE ARE THE RECORDS?
IDEN OF 'SPECIFIC' SAP/SCI ON THE SERVER PROVIDES A TARGET (ROADMAP) TO REVIEW ACCESS LOGS TO THAT SPECIFIC PROGRAM?
WHAT PROCESS AND/OR SEC CLEARANCE WOULD BE REQ TO WALK-AWAY **[TERMINAL_CLEAR]** W/ SAP/SCI MATERIAL 'ELECTRONICALLY'?
Did a Foreign State gain access to the server?
Did a Foreign State gain access to the SAP/SCI material on the server?
(https://bit.ly/2LatWYk).
IF THE TOP FBI CHAIN OF COMMAND FOR THE MIDYEAR INVESTIGATION WERE *ALL* FIRED DOES ONE CONCLUDE THE INVESTIGATION WAS NOT CONDUCTED PROPERLY?
DOES ONE CONCLUDE ALL STATEMENTS MADE BY THE FBI (THINK NO HACK OF SERVER AS SINGLE EXAMPLE) COULD BE

FALSE?
Take a moment and think about what that means.
[   ]
TREASON.
Q

Murdered Agents

On August 29 2018, Independentcitizen.com (https://bit.ly/3ce7xFs) ran a headline "China Murdered 20 CIA Agents After Hacking Hillary's Server." Yes, they did.

But they didn't find those CIA spies by hacking Hillary's servers. They found out because they had access to all Clinton's emails.

Why else would Judicial Watch president Tom Fitton be asking about a gmail address connected to China in some way that was receiving copies of all those thousands of emails in real time?

Why then have the Clintons not been arrested?

I do not know.

All I can surmise is that, as Q stated in his post of February 6 2020, this is "Bigger Than You Can Imagine."

TWO DARK AGENDAS

Sometimes we come across information that we do not want to believe, so it goes on the back burner or down the memory hole, until some time in the future other information comes along that requires one to revisit what one has wanted to discount or even forget.

Such is the case with this trove of information about Obama and Hillary Clinton. She has been a fixture in US politics for decades, while Obama virtually catapulted from anonymity on to the world stage with his election as president in 2008.

What I for one have been slow to accept is that they have both been ideal servants of the New World Order agenda.

Over the years with the advent of a massive amount of information by Q – echoed to some extent by President Trump – and especially because of the deep research by thousands of Qanons and their subsequent memes, a lot of events have been connected and a pattern revealed.

Now imagine a meme topped with an image of Obama on the left, and Hillary on the right.

The headline alongside Obama says "Barack Obama (8yrs). Goal: Weaken USA Globally."

Her headline says "Hillary Clinton (8yrs). Goal: Destroy USA; Rise NWO."

Beneath each of them are small blocks of text, 14 on Obama's side, 12 on hers.

Someone has gone to the trouble of connecting a lot of dots, so to speak, and then created this particular meme.

It visually represents what was to have been a 16-year process of weakening America to the point that the New World Order could finally take over the United States and consolidate its control of the entire globe.

Conquering the United States of America by infiltration rather than invasion was their strategy, because America is, or was, the keystone in their global arch of domination. Without taking over the USA, they could not complete their ambition.

The meme is a disturbing read, and no doubt will be considered fantasy by some, or a "conspiracy theory" by others. But again, what is the NWO agenda, if it is not a conspiracy involving top-level politicians and fellow travelers installed in all intelligence agencies and government departments as a shadow government or as operatives of the Deep State?

Without further comment, here is what that meme spells out.

OBAMA'S AGENDA

- Install Rogue Operators in Government; Comey, Lynch, Holder etc.

- Fund Terrorism (MS13 / ISIS); Control Domestic Terror.

- Leak Classified Intel Military Secrets; Intel to China/Russia.

- Special Access Program Selloff; SAP on Hillary's Servers.

- Nuclearize North Korea and Iran; Blind-eye to Nuke Progress.

- Cut Military Funding; Budget Sequestration.

- Fund/Supply North Korea and Iran; Uranium 1, Iran Deal.

- Target/Weaken Conservative Base; IRS Targeting, MSM Bias.

- Kill NASA Space Supremacy; End Space Shuttle.

- Relax Borders/Flood Illegals; New Dem Voters.

HILLARY'S AGENDA

- World War III / Real and Orchestrated; Planned like WW1-2.

- Revise Constitution; Kill Rights and Freedoms.

- Close US Military Bases Globally; Weaken Military Response.

- Population Control / Pocket Billions $$$; Mass Extinction Event.

- Ban Sale of Firearms (repeal) 2nd Amendment; No Guns/ Armed Revolt.

- Destroy/Censor Opposing News Outlets; FCC Censorship.

- Eliminate Final Good Guys in Government; No Resistance.

- Install Corrupt Supreme Court Justices; Dem/Liberal Legal Wins.

- Open Borders; Endless Supply Dem Voters.

- Kill Economy/Starve/Enslave Public; Starved, Blind & Stupid.

- Remove Electoral College; Rigged Voting Machines.

WE AVOIDED WW3

How close did we come to World War Three?

Don't take my word for it, but if you do your own research, you will find that the Illuminati has literally planned and then instigated virtually every major war in the past 100 years at least.

They owe no allegiance to any country, and are so cold-blooded that the death of millions means nothing to them. Plus they understand the deep lust for power that certain individuals will do anything to gain, or retain.

What else Hillary (aka Killary) might have done had she been elected is open to speculation, and even the agenda itemized above could be seen as only an educated guess in some respects.

However, the way things were at the time she lost, I for one felt that had she been elected, we would have very soon seen some sort of major False Flag event which would have put the US at war with Russia, and more than likely set off World War Three.

Even so, you might recall that North Korea got into a bellicose hissing contest with President Trump. North Korea was firing missiles across the ocean and over Japan; and there was a time when Hawaii itself activated its "incoming missile" alarm system. They would later insist it was all an accidental tripping of the switch.

The truth may well be that North Korea had been an "asset" of the Deep State for decades. Its nuclear ambitions and missile technology were most likely provided to them so they could be constantly seen by the world as a real threat to world peace.

It was a threat that was never resolved by any American president - until Donald Trump got into the White House, and young Kim Jong Un became the leader of North Korea.

False Flag Missile

What I have learned is that the missile that was fired toward Hawaii was intended to be the shot that started WW3 - because ("they" thought) America would have to respond in kind. I can't swear that that is exactly what happened, but it does have a ring of truth to it.

Hillary Clinton can be seen as a powerful politician if you wish. She can also be seen as a wizard at manipulating others, or as a willing puppet with a lust for power that knows no bounds.

As secretary of State, she told those who were willing to go to the aid of Ambassador Stephens when his Benghazi consulate was under attack, to stand down.

They didn't, but many, including the ambassador, died horrible deaths. You can see my full report about "Clinton's Ghosts From Benghazi: on my YouTube channel, if it still exists (https://bit.ly/2XY5wax). It has had over 25,000 views to date.

Killary Klinton was also instrumental in the invasion of Libya and the assassination of Muamar Qaddafi, about which she is on film as saying, in a laughing cackling tone of voice, "we came, we saw, he died."

Do you think she would have had any compunction about starting World War Three so she and her masters could then establish their New World Order?

THE OBAMA RECORD

As for Obama, his track record is on record in regard to most of the items on his bucket list.

As I write (June 4 2020) the Senate is investigating as to how the DOJ and FBI set up the surveillance of Donald Trump's election campaign,. asking why they also targeted a three star general, General Flynn, who had served his country for three decades - with an unblemished record I might add.

Obama is on record as having suggested to incoming President Trump that he should not appoint General Flynn to any role in his new team.

In the Senate hearing, Senator Ted Cruz verbally eviscerated Rod Rosenstein - the guy who signed off on several applications to the Foreign Intelligence Surveillance Court for warrants to do their dirty work.

Cruz made it very clear that President Obama was "at the top" when it came to setting up General Flynn, who was to be President Trump's National Security Adviser.

A Twitter entry from Ronna McDaniel, chairwoman of the GOP, reads:- "@TedCruz completely exposes how Barack Obama and Joe Biden 'unleashed, weaponized, and politicized the Department of Justice, the FBI and the Intelligence Community' to go after @realDonaldTrump" (https://bit.ly/2A2sAwM).

In the hearing, as seen on a video on Twitter, Cruz said "the decision-making to do so went right up to the very top."

Referring to two documents, he pointed out that one of them, dated January 4th 2017, clearly stated that the FBI had closed its investigation into General Flynn. His quote from that document:- "General Flynn was no longer a viable candidate to be part of this larger case. Their investigation did not yield any information on which to predicate further investigative efforts. The FBI is closing this investigation."

The Senator then slammed that document down and in a raised voice said:- "The next day, James Comey, the Director of the FBI, is sitting in the Oval Office with Barack Obama, with Joe Biden, and James Comey, according to a memo from Susan Rice, one of the most remarkable cya (cover-your-ass) memos ever written in Washington, written on her last day in office, and emailed to herself (!!) saying, by the way the investigation into the National Security Adviser coming into the new office, the president has said 'do it by the book.' She says 'by the book' three times. James Comey tells the president 'we're investigating Michael Flynn 'by the book.'

"Well (says Cruz) unless 'the book' is Richard Nixon's Watergate, the day before the FBI said they were closing the investigation and there's James Comey telling Barack Obama we're going after General Flynn, a decorated three-star General, the incoming National Security Adviser to the president, with Joe Biden sitting right there nodding along. Joe Biden himself personally unmasks Michael Flynn's name."

General Flynn, as National Security Adviser, would have seen all the Top Secret reports about how the sting operation against Donald Trump got started in the first place.

Therefore, though Cruz did not say this in so many words, at that meeting in the White House on January 5 2017, during the transition phase, Obama, FBI Director Comey, Vice President Joe Biden, and Susan Rice laid the groundwork that resulted in the fundamentally criminal Flynn takedown.

Subversive Actions

In a Tweet on June 4 2020, President Trump said "FBI and DOJ had NO EVIDENCE to start an investigation against President Trump. @FoxNews "These are people with subversive actions and outright lies. They doctored documents." @jasoninthehouse "Now proven conclusively that this was the political crime of the century!"

Can you imagine that getting any traction in the Deep State/Dem media? I can't.

Whether Obama personally authorized the death of Justice Scalia in February 2016 is another matter entirely, but 79-year-old Scalia definitely died in very questionable circumstances while visiting the Cibolo Creek ranch, which is a long way from anywhere in West Texas. Depending on who you believe his death was either as a result of a pillow over his face while he slept, or natural causes. There was no autopsy.

If Obama had expected to take advantage of Conservative Scalia's death and fill the vacancy with a Liberal-leaning nominee, he failed. The Republican-controlled Senate said because Scalia's death occurred in an election year, they would not even consider any nomination from the president. (https://bit.ly/2WeLDwi).

Consequently, on January 31 2017, just days after his inauguration, President Trump successfully nominated Neil Gorsuch, and, later, Brett Kavanaugh – with all the ferocious opposition by the Deep State involved in that hearing.

By Deep State opposition I mean there were politicians on both sides of the house who were desperate to see that nomination fail. But the failure was theirs.

While the Supreme Court is obviously the highest court in the land, there is an irony in the way that both Republicans and Democrats insist that the court be the preserve of independent individuals who, like Lady Justice herself, are capable of well balanced decisions, coming to conclusions without fear or favor in regard to politics.

That's a joke.

It's just a simple and obvious fact that each party wants to install its own nominees throughout the judiciary in the expectation that their contribution to whatever rulings result in future cases will favor their party's philosophy.

The Democrats for instance would love to see rulings allowing gun confiscation, even to the extent of disarming every citizen in the country, whereas under President Trump, the Second Amendment and the right to bear arms is all but sacrosanct.

DEEP STATE RUNS DEEP

"Conspiracy theorists" have long suspected that the Democrats are about as Deep State as you can get. There is mounting evidence that they are totally correct.

Nor is that judgment reserved simply for politicians such as Pelosi, Biden, Waters, Schiff, Obama and Clinton - and some on the other side of the aisle.

There are many elected positions throughout the country which have been filled by Democrat supporters. Most of them are unknown to the general public, but like Dr Anthony Fauci of the National Institutes of Allergy and Diseases (NIAID) or many judges, they have either been appointed or elected to positions that enable them to play a part in the Deep State sleight of hand shell game.

Democrat governors are also constantly at odds with President Trump, while extending their own versions of tyranny, power and control.

The Democrats are also well known for constantly pushing to outlaw gun ownership. That's because they fear an armed citizenry would rebel to the point of a civil war at some crucial point in their efforts to nullify the US Constitution and have America become part of the New World Order.

Perhaps future generations will look back at archives, such as this book, and understand how close America came to being absorbed into a dark Deep State/Globalist future. Perhaps they will note that the turning point came with the election of Donald Trump, and the following appearance of Q and the Qanons on the Internet and throughout the world.

Judicial Vacancies

But coming back to the present, those Obama/Clinton bucket lists might easily be dismissed as figments of some meme writer's fertile imagination.

What is not a case of imagination is this. When Obama left office, and Clinton failed to replace him, President Trump walked into the White House to find that there were 142 vacancies to be filled in the judicial system. He spoke about this at a televised Town Hall gathering in March 2020.

Those vacancies were in federal courts, the Courts of Appeal, and two on the Supreme Court.
In all, he had appointed 220 judges to various positions.
However, here's the most interesting part. He said that normally, when a new president comes into office, "there are none," meaning that there are no judicial vacancies to be filled.

The obvious question then, is why did Obama leave so many holes in the system? The answer that comes to mind is that this was deliberate. It was (perhaps) an unwritten agreement within the Deep State and between Obama and Clinton, that when she became president, she would then appoint all her own favorites to those vacancies – then generate a variety of controversies that would require court rulings, thereby gilding the NWO agenda with a patina of legality.

For instance, the gun control issue might have seen a few more false flag massacres orchestrated by the Deep State, requiring (according to Democrats and "President" Hillary Clinton) a changed interpretation of the Second Amendment.

What change would that be? Well, perhaps by the time the issue found its way through the various stacked lower courts and eventually to the Supreme Court, if it too were stacked in the Democrats' favor, it might very well reinterpret that amendment to say the right to bear arms was a "collective" right, and not an individual one.

Thankfully, there's no chance of that happening under a Trump presidency.

Footnote:-

Excerpt from Q Post 154 Nov 14 2017.

"Why do D's push for gun control 'directly' after every tragic incident?

"Why is this so very important to their agenda?

"We, the people, are who they are afraid of.

"We, the people, are who they fear will one day awake."

URANIUM ONE

Under President Obama and Secretary of State Hillary Clinton, the Uranium One deal, as it is now known, gave Russia control of 20 per cent of America's uranium.

It was a deal which is summed up in one line of Q's Post 570 of Jan 21 2018 - "U1 fund/supply IRAN/NK [+**reduce US capacity**]."

Spelled out, that means Russia would then be able to process that uranium and pass it on to both Iran and North Korea, while at the same time reducing US capacity and availability.

For the Clintons, setting up the deal was a money windfall. Bill's speech fees certainly picked up once she became Secretary of State. Let's have a look at the facts related to his speech-making appearances.

Bill Clinton was paid $550,000 – that's more than half a million dollars – for just one speech "to a business forum in Shanghai, China, in 2011." (https://bit.ly/2L9t85T).

Following that link, we find an article (https://bit.ly/2A8uDiA) on Politifact (The Poynter Institute) examining claims made in the book *Clinton Cash* by Peter Schweizer.

He writes that "Of the 13 Clinton speeches that fetched $500,000 or more, only two occurred during the years his wife was not secretary of state."

One of them was a 2010 speech in Russia for $500,000, while his wife as Secretary of State was helping Obama to enable Russia to buy a majority stake in Uranium One.

By the way, according to where it is found and extracted, uranium has a specific signature which, no matter how far it is processed, can be used to identify exactly where it came from.

What if "She" Won?

Once again I find myself wondering what would surely have happened to our world if "she" had won. Nuclear war? Yet another devastating false flag such as a premeditated attack on the US by either Iran or North Korea, forcing the US to respond in kind?

Then comes a great sigh of relief, and gratitude, for what President Trump has done to rein in North Korea, cripple Iran's nuclear ambitions, and, though not so obvious, create what appears to be a very different relationship with both Kim Jong Un of North Korea and Vladimir Putin of Russia.

"America For Sale"

The Teflon Twins and their Clinton Foundation have long been under scrutiny, and at some point all will be revealed, including details behind what an FBI note calls "crimes against children."

For the moment, based on the details Q and Qanon researchers have uncovered, it is no wonder that Q has posted about the Hillary/China/emails connection, and made the statement:- "America For Sale."

Take this Q Post 3837 of February 6 2020, for example.
BIGGER THAN YOU CAN IMAGINE.
More than selling of State Secrets.

More than selling of US security.
More than selling of MIL tech.
More than selling of C_A assets. *(That involved the revealing to China of the names of CIA assets in that country, all of whom were believed to have been eliminated – killed or imprisoned – though Q would later suggest that some escaped that purge.)*
More than selling of NSA bulk data collection programs.
More than selling of Uranium.
More than selling of US Space NAT SEC programs & positions.
More than selling of US AID..
More than selling of SAPs
CLAS 1-99
....
>Crimes against Humanity.
When you cannot destroy/defeat the United States of America by attacking head on, you change tactics and deploy a 'KILL FROM WITHIN' **[internal]** operation.
>Financial/Economy
>Military/Police
>Division of Citizenry
>Border Collapse
[Install 'like-minded' leaders in key positions of US Gov]
How many people **[removed]** from the FBI had Iranian family backgrounds?
The Silent War Continues.....
Q

It's in the public record that President Obama sent five planeloads of cash to Iran, and that his closest adviser, Valerie Jarrett, was born in Iran. Huma Abedin's father is Iranian. Abedin was Hillary Clinton's close friend and confidant for decades. Peter Strzok's father was Iranian, as was Lisa Page's mother.

Both were removed from the FBI for their part in setting up the Russia collusion hoax.

HOW THEY DO IT

In contemplating the enormity of the Toronto Protocols I had to ask myself, how do they do it? How do they do it, and get away with it?

Naturally, the answer of choice is that "they" are scumbags, a living virus in human form that is driven to consume and destroy the very host that allows it to live.

The other answer, equally unpalatable for some, is that we as individuals have allowed ourselves to just go along with the crowd, or the herd, or the flock. Some are more comatose than others, but as this Great Awakening gathers more and more momentum, many tens of thousands are starting to really see how close we came to the slaughterhouse (metaphorically speaking).

Because I've been studying these bacteria for a long time, it actually wasn't too difficult to come up with a list of the ways they have done what they've done.

If you're not familiar with the process, you can join me now and do some research about just a few examples, with source links and keyword suggestions as we go.

RESEARCH EXERCISE

Here is an exercise in researching some of the everyday items and chemicals that have been created and marketed by the Globalist cartel.

We're going to look at Teflon, Aluminum, Fluoride and Chemtrails, all of which I have investigated over the past many years, but which are worth a fresh look considering our interest in the Globalists' cunning ways.

Teflon:-

Search keywords- Teflon DuPont Settlement (because I watched a movie that brought this to my attention).

On the first page of the search results, we find:- "A new Netflix documentary (https://bit.ly/3dhIq4G) titled, *"The Devil We Know,"* tells the story of DuPont's decades-long cover-up of the harm caused by chemicals used to make its popular non-stick Teflon™ products. The film shows how the chemicals used to make Teflon poisoned people and the environment – not just in Parkersburg, West Virginia, where DuPont had a Teflon plant, but all over the world."

I haven't seen that video, but I did watch another film, *"Dark Waters,"* made in 2019, which dramatizes attorney Robert Bilott's case against DuPont after they contaminated a town water supply with unregulated chemicals. It happened in the 1960s.

After finding mice had some bad reactions to Teflon, DuPont gave staff cigarettes laced with Teflon as a human trial. Women either aborted or gave birth to malformed children.

Others in the town aborted, bore deformed children, or died of cancer. DuPont denied culpability for many years, but eventually paid a $671 million settlement in a class action case. Yet Teflon still appears in everything from cookware to clothing.

I check several sites when doing a search, and then I opt to quote from the one that has the most common sense about it.

In this case, ACHNews is a blog by a woman, a mother, who says on her About page (https://bit.ly/3fqCZ5b), "I am a mother of two beautifully free children who run around in the forests and creeks of North Carolina.

"I am passionate about the health of this Home we call Earth. I sit at the feet of birthing mothers and serve their nesting-postpartum time. I care for children and their parents. I strive to live in balance with an awareness of what I am leaving behind for children's great-grandchildren."

The headline on the blog article (https://bit.ly/3b8Cutn) written by Annie Kin and published on December 12 2019 says:- "Teflon: DuPont, EPA and the Pentagon Covered Up the Mass Poisoning of America."

Kin writes:- "According to test results from the federal Centers for Disease Control and Prevention, 98 percent of Americans have PFAS in their blood.

"Even at very low doses, PFAS chemicals in drinking water have been linked to an increased risk of cancer, reproductive and immune system harm, harm to the liver, thyroid disease and other health problems."

I have a very strong feeling that is because the Environmental Protection Agency (EPA), which is supposed to regulate chemicals in the environment, has been infiltrated by the Deep State.

A fine of $671 million would be nothing but small change to a company making $1 billion a year off Teflon products in the 1960s.

Why would I say the EPA has been infiltrated? Because the EPA, instead of banning the use of these poisons, has been shown to be more than lenient in its assessment of "safe" levels of such toxins.

Then, when disease strikes, the corporations can all hide behind plausible deniability because of the agency's determination of "safe" levels of these inorganic compounds. The thought of "depopulation by stealth" comes to mind.

Aluminum:-

This one is important because of its relationship to fluoride, chemtrails, Alzheimers disease, and wildfires.
My search keywords – Aluminum+Health+brain.

A variety of articles both pro and con appear on the first page of results. Most say aluminum affects the brain and has been linked to Alzheimers. One study showed "unsafe and high amounts of aluminum" in the brains of five autistic individuals – higher than levels found in cases like Alzheimers.

I then try a keyword phrase - When did Alzheimers start. Not very productive, but the disorder was named after Alois Alzheimer from his studies circa 1901.

I should add that there is surely a difference between a "disorder" and a "disease." I'm thinking right now that "disorders" are induced by a chemical imbalance, while a "disease" is a consequence of bugs successfully attacking a badly maintained or compromised immune system. (Just a thought to ponder.)

I then try a keyword phrase – Alzheimers bell curve chart. (Nothing useful unless you want to use Excel spreadsheets.)
Try again. Keywords – Alzheimers statistics. This brings me to alzheimers.net (https://bit.ly/3fpYgMl).
In the United States,
- Alzheimer's is the 6th leading cause of death
- the only disease in the 10 leading causes of deaths in the United States that cannot be cured, prevented or slowed.
- 1 in 10 Americans over the age of 65 has Alzheimer's.
- There was an 89% increase in deaths due to Alzheimer's between 2000 and 2014.
- More than 5 million Americans are living with Alzheimer's.
- By 2050, it's estimated there will be as many as 16 million Americans living with Alzheimer's.
- By 2025, the number of people aged 65 and older with Alzheimer's disease is expected to reach 7.1 million people, a 27% increase from the 5.6 million age 65 and older in 2019.
- By 2050, there could be as many as 7 million people age 85 and older with Alzheimer's disease, accounting for half (51%) of all people 65 and older with Alzheimer's.

Fluoride:-

Keywords – Fluoride+health+effects.

MedicalNewsToday (https://bit.ly/3fwPGM6) tells us "fluoride is a neurotoxin which in high doses can be harmful."

Arguments for and against its addition to drinking water have been going on since Day One. It was "sold" like many other authoritarian impositions, on the grounds that it was "safe," and that above all, it would fight the scourge of dental caries, thereby preventing tooth decay.

I am supposed to believe that a neurotoxin can prevent tooth decay? Or does it decay nerves and neurons?
And what about this – dentists are still busy every day, making as much as $700,000 a year – and up to $1 million a year if they're specialists.

Personally, I like Dr Mercola and his thoroughly researched articles, like this one on Fluoride (https://bit.ly/3fwOIzs). "Fluoride is a toxic industrial waste product, which may also be contaminated with lead, arsenic, radionucleotides, aluminum and other industrial contaminants. The fluoride added to municipal water supplies is not pharmaceutical grade."

So why is it in water and toothpaste etc? Because it is a neurotoxin, and reduces IQ levels – and because the Cabal controls the pharmaceutical industry, most of the medical community, and because they don't just want sheep, they want really dumb sheep who will die off earlier than they should because they're no longer useful.

Fluoride in combination with other nanoparticles helps them achieve that result.

CHEMTRAILS

The subject of chemtrails deserves its own deep research because of its global role in the Deep State eugenics operation.

Keywords – "best chemtrail site." Okay, in the results we find Huffpost huffing about "conspiracy theory websites" and "research to debunk chemtrail claims."

But on globalskywatch.com (my first visit) I'm told that "Chemtrails are plumes emitted by aircraft that have been determined to contain highly-toxic metals that are harmful to all life. *This historic issue affects everyone.*"

And "High Bypass Turbofans Don't Produce Trails. (https://bit.ly/2W8PquW) "Jet engines on commercial and military aircraft are not capable of producing trails. So what are those lines in the sky?"

Personally, I'd always thought contrails (as opposed to chemtrails) were simply a result of the plane flying through cold air. Their exhaust interacted with the cold air, caused a white trail behind the plane, and that trail gradually dissolved. It didn't spread. It just dissolved.

Having just learned that jet engines do not produce trails, I guess I was looking at prop-driven planes like the DC3 which were passenger planes in New Zealand before they upgraded to things like Fokker Friendships and consigned the DC3s to the role of crop dusting.

(I made a documentary back in New Zealand for TV One's popular Country Calendar program about that. A DC3 is an awesome bird. In fact, a friend and I once considered buying a stretched DC3 to fly North to Inner Earth... oops...getting sidetracked here).

Chemtrails Real

Honestly, although I hadn't visited this chemtrail site until now, I have done a lot of research on the subject over the years. You can draw your own, but my conclusions are that chemtrails are real. I have personally taken photos of them from my own home in Washington state, and watched the trail spread sideways and become a misty cloud cover.

In one respect, chemtrails are openly associated with military efforts to control the weather. The military has even talked about that to the Senate. Search "military geoengineering patents" and you'll find they have many patents on the process. There is one for Rolls Royce (https://bit.ly/2BhPWPk) that uses an electromagnetic generator to make contrails invisible so artificial clouds do not develop.

That means whatever is in those invisible contrails is exactly that - invisible.
Despite the huffing and puffing and truth deniers, it is very clear that the Deep State uses this technology for very ulterior motives.

Chemtrails contain nano-particles of a variety of minerals. Among them is aluminum. Why?

Chemtrails have been recorded countless times over California, and they have also been sprayed over much of Australia.

A video I watched, presented by an Aussie, included the information that the aluminum particles are exactly the same as what is used in fireworks known as "sparklers." You know, the little fizzy thing you can hold in your hand and spin around and make exciting images in the air around the bonfire.

BUT – spray those nano-particles onto already dry countryside, and if and when a fire starts, by whatever means, those aluminum particles explode just like those sparkler fireworks, and in doing so force that fire to spread extremely rapidly.

The "Opportune Moment"

You might suspect that I'm going off on a tangent here, but can you imagine how handy that would be for a technically bankrupt state like California, especially if its state and national politicians were Globalist fellow travelers?

You could start by having "experts" introduce the concept of Global Warming and your media lackeys would pound on that narrative relentlessly.

Then you could have your friends use their weather modification technology to create a series of droughts which your citizens would believe were just a consequence of your Global Warming scam. Meanwhile those aluminum nanoparticles along with every other debilitating ingredient in those chemtrails would be sprayed over specially selected areas.

Then, as the pirate Captain Jack Sparrow would say, you wait for the "opportune moment." If, perchance, you have a laser cannon hovering out of sight up in space, or (perhaps more realistically) a helicopter or two fitted with the right sort of lasers, you could fire at will and light a series of fires almost simultaneously in a large suburb. Thousands would be forced to evacuate. A state of emergency would be declared. The Federal government could then be milked for millions if not billions of dollars in disaster relief.

Assuming that worked, but your rapid transit rail system was going nowhere fast (pun intended) why not ignite a series of major forest fires, regardless of how they might completely destroy small towns. Your opportune moment would be when the Santa Anna winds (or whatever they're called) are blowing relentlessly. You tell the public you fear that this will cause power lines to collapse and start fires, shut down the grid, blame the fires on Pacific Power's lack of maintenance, and milk the Federal government for even more.

Imminent Demise

Call all that a fantasy if you wish, but for myself, when it comes to the Illuminati and their Dark Agenda, which they have been perfecting and implementing for millennia, I consider nothing to be beyond the bounds of possibility - including the fact that their demise is imminent. Unfortunately, that will take a year or two yet, and the human consequences of their deliberate slow motion eugenics plan, which does involve chemtrails and aluminum particles, will linger for some time to come.

The reason is that when that chemtrail cocktail is sprayed over populated areas, the populace has no choice but to ingest it with every breath. In addition, if that aluminum in minute form settles on any area that is an aquifer for a city, it will inevitably find its way into the city water supply.

And then what? Then it combines with the fluoride neurotoxin with which the water has already been treated. People drink the city water (ignoring the taste of chlorine) unaware that aluminum and fluoride bonded together in such minute quantities are in reality a more potent neurotoxin. And then there is an increase over time in dementia and Alzheimer's disease.

DEATH AND DENIAL

"**N**obody gets out of this alive" is a saying that in the past has appealed to my dark humor side. Much darker than that, however, is the quip that "nothing is certain but death and taxes."

It just makes you wonder, who made that up? The Controllers maybe? After all, as far as they're concerned, we're only really good for our vote, which gives them power, and our taxes, which gives them more power.

However, from their point of view, like sheep, we have a predictable life span, and we become useless eaters after a certain point. As far as they're concerned, even though they have stripped so many of us of morals and ethics, made sex of any kind the meaning of life and love, and introduced eugenics via Planned Parenthood and abortion on demand, it seems like they're worried about us over-populating the planet.

There is indisputable evidence that they have been responsible for the deaths of millions in the wars and false flag events they have planned and executed (bad pun intended). Why then would they not expand their thinking – just as we should expand ours – but in their case, come up with a multitude of ways to cull the population, while making money off it at the same time?

Frankly, I never had thoughts like that, at least not in such detail, until recently. As a reporter covering agriculture at one time, I did stories about how crop sprays were totally bad and people had to wear full hazmat suits while spraying their orchards because of the carcinogens in the stuff they were spraying.

Baby - Floor - Cancer

Certainly, there are other reasons why cancer gets a grip. But where does the propensity for its eventual appearance start? In some cases it may be genetic, in that it is latent in the DNA until some future event triggers the cancer into activity.

As a metaphor you could say it is akin to a hidden enemy crafting a roadside bomb which just sits there doing nothing until that point in time when events and circumstances converge. The blast kills some instantly, others slowly, and a few survive.

Q dropped quite a bit of cryptic information about the Globalist agenda in
Q Post 1010 of April 4 2018. You can find it on qmap.pub under the search term "baby on floor" and headed Money, Power and Control:-
MONEY.
POWER.
CONTROL.
People are simply in the way.
SLAVES.
SHEEP.
PAWNS.
MASS EXT EVENTS DESIGNED TO DECREASE THREAT LEVEL OF POPULATION.
GUN CONTROL.
WARS **[FAKE][TOP HAPPY][BACKEND DEAL]**.
ELECTION RIGGING.
CONTROL.
YOUR VOICE DOES NOT MATTER.
PHARMA **[CLAS-D]**

WATER
AIR
CHEMICALS PUSHED FOR HOME USE CLEANING **[CANCER]**
[BABY ON FLOOR-HANDS IN MOUTH – THE START].
VACCINES **[NOT ALL]**.
TOBACCO.
OPIOIDS.
ULTIMATE WIN **[DEATH + MONEY]**.
THE FED.
ROTHSCHILD.
'CONSPIRACY'
'CONSPIRACY'
'CONSPIRACY'
UK/GER **[5 days]**.
Choice is yours.
REVELATIONS.
ENOUGH IS ENOUGH.
Q

The words "CHEMICALS PUSHED FOR HOME USE CLEANING [CANCER][BABY ON FLOOR-HANDS IN MOUTH – THE START]," had plenty of Qanons confused, one of whose queries was later posted and answered by Q.

The question was "Did anons ever figure out what Q meant with the 'baby on floor hands in mouth – the start.' Was this Syria FF?"

No, it was a long way from referencing the faked chemical attacks in Syria – faked by the Deep State in order to allow its toady governments to start another war – which again is another story.

Q's response to that query was, "Finally. Chemicals. Learn our comms."

He was saying basically that "we drop the crumbs of information. You make the bread," which means work it out for yourself; think it through; make connections; use logic, and so forth.

In this case, there was a logical connection between "chemicals" and "baby on floor." The totally innocent unsuspecting mother has washed the floor clean so her baby doesn't ingest any germs. Little does she know that the chemicals she has used leave a residue, even when dry, and the baby gets them on its hands, which, as happens with all babies, at some point find their way into its mouth.

Like a roadside bomb, those chemicals lay in wait in the body, until that future time when there is a convergence and cancer explodes into death-dealing action.

KILLER CHEMICALS

Q has often said "these people are sick."

How true is that! They are so sick that through their control of the chemical, pharmaceutical and medical industries they make millions off the sick and dying.

Now when it comes to the Protocols, consider this. "They" control the mainstream medical business, from education to implementation, as well as the pharmaceutical industry, not to mention research into all diseases including cancer. It is a multi-billion-dollar industry, and the profits are astronomical.

Is it any wonder that no cure for cancer has ever been revealed? Is it any wonder that they despise those who are specialists in alternative methodologies, such as homeopathy, vitamin supplements, and so forth? Is it a suspicious thing that many doctors who have advocated natural remedies have died by accident – or "suicide"?

How little do those thousands of dedicated care givers know about the reality – their industry is designed to make money for the elite from the sick and dying – including those whose cancer resulted from ingesting minute particles of household cleaners while crawling on mother's clean floor.
Was Q just making that up?
No.

Clean floors are not the only problem when it comes to unknowingly ingesting inorganic chemicals in the home. From Science News Feb 21 2019 (https://bit.ly/2YH2n0E):- "Chemicals called semivolatile organic compounds have been linked to health problems.

"Children who grow up in houses with all vinyl flooring or living room sofas that contain flame retardants called PBDEs have higher levels of potentially harmful chemicals in their bodies than other kids, a study finds."

That being so, if and when these chemicals fulfill their potential for harm, the victim and the makers of those chemicals will be so far removed from the initial cause that it would be impossible to make let alone prove a valid connection. Hence the term, "plausible deniability."

Unfortunately, the same seems to go for everything underhanded the Globalists and their corporations, not to mention puppet politicians at every level from national to local, get into.

MONSANTO

The first three returns in a search for "Monsanto etiology" tell us that it has admitted disguising a $50,000 bribe to an Indonesian environment minister related to its genetically modified cotton.

We also discover that a California man has been awarded $80 million because he got cancer using Monsanto's Roundup weedkiller; that the company manipulated scientific studies; and that 17 scientists have spoken out about Roundup causing cancer.

Monsanto was acquired by the German company Bayer in a $63 billion dollar takeover, but Bayer still has to cope with Roundup-related law suits from more than 13,000 farmers, landscapers and gardeners. And that's just in the USA.

One link takes us to a half-truth (fake really) headline that says "Bayer gets help from Donald Trump as US regulators veto warnings its Roundup weedkiller causes cancer."

The online article by Markets Insider (https://bit.ly/2SI3nxV) has nothing to do with the president personally, but the headline probably served well as clickbait.

What it reveals is that the federal Environmental Protection Agency Administrator Andrew Wheeler has refused to approve a proposal that product labels should warn that glyphosate – Roundup's active ingredient – causes cancer. California has required such labeling since 2017. Wheeler said "It is irresponsible to require labels on products that are inaccurate. We will not allow California's flawed program to dictate federal policy."

Hopefully at some point Wheeler's EPA will revisit the science surrounding Roundup and glyphosate.
Monsanto's Roundup pesticide is still not banned, even though court cases in the past couple of years have resulted in multi-million-dollar settlements because it has caused cancers and other serious health effects.

Corn(ered) Market

Genetically modified corn is the one making headlines because Monsanto has cornered the market by requiring farmers to buy corn seed only from them – the GMO variety. Try keywords GMO+corn and you'll find a Newsweek article (https://bit.ly/2YH5ghT) saying "GMO Corn Is Safe and Even Has Health Benefits...." (I'd suggest keeping in mind that the mainstream media is mostly owned by the globalists.

They also control the world's food chains, as noted in the Toronto Protocols.) Moving on to eatingwell.com (https://bit.ly/3fvb43Y) (my first visit) we find an undated article:- "Introduced in the mid-1990s, genetically modified (GMO) seeds now produce nearly 90 percent of the field corn in the United States (along with more than 90 percent of the soy and canola).

(Ed. Note:- Field corn is primarily used for stock feed and production of ethanol, corn syrup etc. Sweet corn is preferred for human consumption.) "Unlike hybridized plants, which are created through cross-pollination, genetically modified plants have strands of DNA added to achieve desired characteristics.

"And in late 2011, Dow Agrichemical upped the stakes with field corn by applying for permission from the FDA to market

GMO corn that is resistant to 2, 4-D, a herbicide that was a component in the Vietnam War-era herbicide Agent Orange and is still used in many home lawn-care products.

"In people who work with 2, 4-D, the chemical has been linked to cancers, hormonal disruptions, reproductive difficulties and birth defects, according to the US. Department of Labor. In wheat-growing states where 2, 4-D and related pesticides are used in large quantities, the Environmental Protection Agency has found higher-than-normal rates of circulatory and respiratory birth defects."

"This summer for the first time, farmers are planting Monsanto's newly approved, genetically modified Performance sweet-corn seeds. Monsanto is aiming its marketing muscle at iconic corn on the cob.

"The new corn has been bio-engineered to survive applications of glyphosate (sold under the trade name Roundup), an herbicide that destroys competing weeds. Monsanto has also spliced genes into the corn ... from Bacillus thuringiensis (Bt) ... Fatal to insect larvae, most experts say Bt is harmless to humans and animals.

However, Canadian researchers reported in 2011 in the journal Reproductive Toxicology that they found residues of Bt in the blood of mothers and fetuses."I have also read that wheat farmers are in the habit of spraying their crops with glyphosate shortly before harvest because it causes the wheat to increase the size of its berries, and hence increase the yield.

But that surely means traces of glyphosate are then introduced to the food chain for human consumption. What are the consequences at the human cellular level?

GMO SUICIDES

It turns out that GMO cotton, rather than corn, figures in reports about suicides in India.

The story is that Monsanto's introduction of modified cotton seed has upped the annual rate of suicides by farmers trapped in a cycle of debt trying to make a living by growing Monsanto's Bt cotton.

In a 2014 article Naturalsociety.com (https://bit.ly/2YGSakR) reported as many as 291,000 suicides since the introduction of GMO cotton seeds in 1992 – most suicides involving ingestion of the herbicide Roundup. If my calculator is accurate, that's an average of 13,000 suicides a year.

Available graphs show suicide rates among farmers have dropped progressively, while hectares in cotton continue to rise, the argument apparently being that there is no relationship between suicides and the production of Bt or GMO cotton.

There is another way to interpret such charts and that would be say that most of those inclined to suicide have already committed the act, which automatically reduces the percentage of those likely to do so in future, which in turn means the drop-off in suicides as portrayed on such charts, is really a "false positive." But it looks good for Monsanto.

TRIFFIDS AND OVENS

First, where would we be without microwave towers spread like Triffids across the landscape, Triffids being those towering alien people-eating monster plants from John Wyndham's 1951 book, *Day Of The Triffids*.

The film version had them trying to munch down on Tom Cruise. However, knowing what we know now, could it be that the book itself was a deliberate work of fiction, but intended to prepare people of the time for the coming of microwave towers?

As for the triffid habit of killing and eating humans, was that a subtle warning that the microwave towers of the future would have a side-effect of killing human brain cells – devouring them, so to speak, or killing some with brain cancers if exposed to certain levels of microwaves?

I'm sure you can find a lot of information about cell towers and health effects if you choose to do a search on the subject, but for now, let's move on to microwave ovens.

Keywords Microwave+oven+health.

Medicaldaily.com (https://bit.ly/2ysanbn) will give you five reasons why microwave oven cooking is harming your health. It destroys breast milk (so don't put those in there) and Vitamin B-12 in beef, pork and milk.

The World Health Organization (WHO) (https://bit.ly/3bb2CUu) will tell you microwaves are contained within the oven when cooking, and "leakage around and through the glass door is limited by design to a level well below that recommended by international standards." (Question to self – Do those who set the standards have any connection to the NWO or Illuminati agenda?)

Keywords – Microwaves + Russia.

Years ago, probably in the 1970s, I was told Russia had banned microwave ovens because of studies raising health concerns. In this search I find they were banned in 1976, but the ban was lifted in the 90s, which is a good example of how a long-held belief can be out of sync with current reality. Even so, I have never trusted official standards and as a matter of choice I have never used microwave ovens.

If you find yourself now questioning other things that come to mind based on your personal experience or concerns, it's easy enough to do a search and look through the available pro and con information that comes up.

Now it's time to move on to another form of population management. If you controlled social media, could you not then formulate all sorts of strategies to further your own ambitions? Strategies like using subliminal messages to influence an election ? Yes. That has been done, by Google and Facebook and Twitter.

DARPA = FB = DS

Is Facebook a Deep State social monitoring and engineering platform? Yes.

How can I say "yes" so emphatically? Because there is a very curious same-day relationship between the date on which Facebook was founded, and a DARPA project called Lifelog being terminated. DARPA has a long history of high tech wizardry, much of which is totally classified, so we have to go with what is available publicly.

Search keyword – DARPA. "The Defense Advanced Research Projects Agency (DARPA) is an agency of the United States Department of Defense responsible for the development of emerging technologies for use by the military. (https://bit.ly/3bdPP3k).

One such project was Combat Zones That See (https://bit.ly/35IHiEv): "track everything that moves" in a city by linking up a massive network of surveillance cameras.

Another was "Intelligent Integration of Information ... database research (which) with ARPA CISTO and NASA, funded the National Science Foundation's Digital Library program, that led to Google."

And "On February 4, 2004 the agency shut down its so-called" LifeLog Project." The project's aim would have been, "to gather in a single place just about everything an individual says, sees or does."

As we'll see in Q's Post 2988 of March 6 2019, which starts with a link (https://bit.ly/2yA7wNr):-
Define 'Lifelog' **[DARPA]**
"an ontology-based (sub)system that captures, stores, and makes accessible the flow of one person's experience in and interactions with the world in order to support a broad spectrum of associates/assistants and other system capabilities."

The objective of the LifeLog concept was "to be able to trace the 'threads' of an individual's life in terms of events, states, and relationships", and it has the ability to "take in all of a subject's experience, from phone numbers dialed and e-mail messages viewed to every breath taken, step made and place gone".

Define 'FB'.
The Facebook service can be accessed from devices with Internet connectivity, such as personal computers, tablets and smartphones. After registering, users can create a customized profile revealing information about themselves. Users can post text, photos and multimedia of their own devising and share it with other users as "friends". Users can use various embedded apps, and receive notifications of their friends' activities. Users may join common-interest groups.
Compare & Contrast.
DARPA senior employees > FB?
DARPA TERMINATES PROGRAM FEB 4, 2004.
FB FOUNDED FEB 4, 2004.
DARPA = FB
Q.

All of which is DS = Deep State.

ELECTION FRAUD

From July 20 2019, on 100percentfedup.com (https://bit.ly/3bf6MdM):- LIBERAL Top Psychologist Testifies: How Google and Facebook Manipulate Votes For Democrats... Can Swing 2020 Election By 15 MILLION Votes.

"Former editor-in-chief of Psychology Today, Dr. Robert Epstein, testified in a Senate Judiciary Committee about how liberal tech giants like Google and Facebook have manipulated, and will likely (https://bit.ly/3fyTSej) continue to manipulate votes for Democrats.

He also warned that in 2020, the invisible manipulation by companies like Google will be like nothing we've ever seen.

How right he was. On May 5 2020 Q's Post 4112 included this quote from a Facebook release. (https://bit.ly/3corKbq). "We removed 5 Pages, 20 Facebook accounts, and 6 Groups that originated in the US and focused domestically.

"Our investigation linked this activity to individuals associated with the QAnon network known to spread fringe conspiracy theories. We found this activity as part of our internal investigations into suspected coordinated inauthentic behavior ahead of the 2020 election in the US." To which Q added "Information Warfare. Q."

In his testimony, Epstein admitted he openly supported Hillary Clinton in the 2016 election, but he also said "I believe in democracy, and I believe in a free and fair election more than I have any kind of allegiance to a candidate or a party.

Senator Cruz read from Dr. Epstein's testimony: "Google's manipulation of votes gave at least 2.6 million additional votes to Hillary Clinton in the year 2016." Cruz asked, "Is that correct?' Epstein answered, "That's correct."

Dr. Epstein clarified that the 2.6 million votes Google moved to Hillary was a 'rock bottom' number, saying that the actual number of votes moved in the direction of Hillary Clinton was closer to a range of 2.6 to 10.4 million votes.

"And the methods that they're using are invisible, they're subliminal. They're more powerful than most any effects I've ever seen in the behavioral sciences, and I've been in the behavioral sciences for over 40 years.

"In 2020, if all these were supporting the same candidate, there are **15 million votes on the line** *that could be shifted without people's knowledge and without leaving a paper trail for authorities to trace.'* Dr. Epstein told Cruz."

At this point my mind recalls something I read a while back and opens a note somewhere in my brain. The memory says "Epstein wife killed." It happened sometime after his testimony appearance.

Using those keywords, a Fox News report (https://fxn.ws/3coDhYF) reveals that his wife died from injuries received in a car crash when she (reportedly) lost control on an I5 on-ramp in California, careened into traffic, and was T-boned by a semi truck.

In a number of entries on Twitter after her death, Epstein would say "Last year, after I briefed a group of state AGs about

#Google's power to rig elections,(https://bit.ly/3cdkVcW) one of them said, 'I think you're going to die in an accident in a few months.'

"A few months later, my beautiful wife #Misti (https://bit.ly/3fCxiRY) died a violent death. Makes you wonder."

He would also tweet "BTW, although losing Misti is devastating for me – there will never be another Misti in my life, after all – I AM STILL NOT SUICIDAL. Hear that, #Google? Hear that, #Hillary?"

And in another Tweet:- "And no, I don't think #Google or #Hillary had anything to do with Misti's death, but for you conspiracy theorists out there, here's a recent article about Misti's accident from one of the world's largest online tabloid newspapers, the @DailyMail. (https://bit.ly/2Wyi87n).

....

Regarding Facebook, d'you think Facebook just might have a role to play in an organization that wants total control of billions of people so it can convince them of the need for a New World Order.

Or do you think Facebook was created by a bored uni student who just wanted to stay in touch with his classmates?

Censorship Rampant

That said, what's very obvious at present is that outfits like Facebook, Google, Instagram and YouTube are all in one way or another censoring input that doesn't gel with the Democrat party's agenda, which, stripped to the bone, is the NWO agenda.

Proof that such corporations are agents of the Deep State is in the fact that they have banned so many accounts that favor

President Trump.

In fact, as this "information warfare" (Q Post 3958, April 14 2020) ramps up during the 2020 election cycle, Q predicted in Post 3957 of the same date that [removal **[blackout] coming of pro_POTUS accounts**].

How does that fit with the Toronto Protocols? It fits very well, for the protocols were all about manipulating humanity on a grand scale.

With its millions, perhaps billions of users Facebook has been one of their data mining facilities which enables them to not only gather intimate details about every user, but also provides them a platform through which to manipulate public opinion, including the way people vote.

EDUCATION – OBAMA $$$

The Illuminati have done a great disservice to humanity through their insidious control of the education system.

You can live through a lot of election cycles in 75 years, and what becomes very clear is that the "reforms" the politicians talk about, and then enact, take what was once a silk purse and turn it into a sow's ear.

You can also realize, especially as a journalist who has sometimes worked close up with politicians during an election, that they can be as slippery as eels, as cunning as snakes, and underneath the smiles and fancy words that in many ways hypnotize their ardent believers, totally corrupt.

Which brings us to Barack Obama and the American education system.

The point I'm making here is that, when seen in light of the Toronto Protocols, every time politicians say they must reform the education system, their true intention is to UNDER-educate students; to ensure that successive generations are less and less informed, and more and more ignorant of such things as the Constitution, the Bill of Rights, ethics, morals, honesty, and personal responsibility for getting along in life.

Worse still, they are burdened with student loans which puts them into debt for years to come while they are being "educated" (read that as "brainwashed") along the lines of the Illuminati agenda. It's almost got to the stage where it's a matter of "get a degree... get a job... at McDonalds."

Have I made the point that the education system has been surreptitiously undermined and downgraded, deliberately? I hope so.

However, to be specific, we only need to search for articles about the Common Core project that Obama all but forced schools to adopt, and how he personally benefited from it financially. No doubt you never saw this on the Corrupt News Network (CNN), but there were some reports that Obama had been given a huge advance on a forthcoming book; $65 million in fact.

Search keywords:- Obama Common Core $65MIL.

"Obama Gave Contract To Common Core Publisher, and Later Got a $65-Million Book Deal. Critics Claim Obama Accepted a Bribe." That's the headline in needtoknownews, (https://bit.ly/3bcL8Xu) December 2019. It goes on:- "Obama recently bought a mansion in Martha's Vineyard for $11.75 million, and also owns homes in Washington, DC and Chicago, and possibly Hawaii.

$65m Kickback

"Ostensibly, Obama's wealth comes mainly from his book deals. Investment Watch reported that he gave Pearson Publishing $350-million to create Common Core book text. In return, Pearson, through its subsidiary, Penguin Random House, gave Obama a $65-million dollar book deal in 2017. In another example, Obama's stance on net neutrality greatly benefited Netflix. Later, Obama was given a lucrative deal with the entertainment company. -GEG"

Yes, for Obama, the education system was a windfall to the tune of many millions of dollars.

Elsewhere you'll find that Common Core had never been tested, and while it was supposed to be introduced voluntarily by the states, many refused, and others dropped out after its introduction. Common Core, by the way, was championed by Microsoft's Bill Gates; Bill Gates being an ardent Globalist himself.

Back in 2018, newspunch reported the results of a study involving the Cato Institute. From just one paragraph:- "Declaring Obama's Common Core to be *"worst large-scale educational failure in 40 years,"* the study examined the effects of Common Core on school choice and found the program has *'blunted the innovation, dynamism, and competition'* while also producing the worst math scores in generations."

It is no wonder that President Trump would lash out at the Obama book deal.

In July 2019 he called for a probe (https://bit.ly/3dnoJIx) into how it came about. So far, that hasn't happened and the Obamas are at this time enjoying their retirement in their new mansion in the Hamptons. Or Hawaii? Or Indonesia? Or somewhere.

To recap, the Toronto Protocols called for what amounts to the dumbing down of students, which has resulted in the production of young adults with an incomplete grasp of history and mathematics, and no knowledge at all of how they have been short-changed.

They are the poorer because of those changes imposed by the likes of Obama, while the likes of Obama have become much wealthier through backdoor deals.

There are other examples of Obama enacting changes in the education world that echo what the Protocols had in mind. For instance, he issued a directive requiring all public schools in the country to allow transgender students access to single sex bathrooms.

Family Fracturing

He used the Race To The Top program to establish more preschool programs – meaning more children spending more time away from their parents, in turn meaning more progress toward the goal of fracturing the family unit.

And he took control of the student loan system by cutting private banks out of the loop so the loans were only available from government sources; more money for the government, more government control of a person's life; exactly what the Protocols and the Illuminati are all about.

As corrupt as Obama's actions have been, he was also said by Joan Rivers, shortly before her unexpected death, to be a homosexual married to a "tranny."

Whatever his sexual preferences might be, they pale when it comes to what must be the most vile Cabal "business" of all – Human trafficking.

They traffic men women and children for slave labor, slave sex, and child abuse of the absolutely worst possible kind.

TRADING CHILDREN

What we as decent human beings would call depravity, is nothing but business as usual for those involved in human trafficking.

It's a big business. A really BIG business.

Those who are at the top of the Illuminati pyramid are not stupid people. Disgusting as it might be to us, the protocols blueprint could be seen as a work of dark genius; a dark agenda that was progressively implemented step by step over a period of many generations.

While they are most certainly bad and evil, they were definitely not stupid enough to reveal the worst of their plans in the Toronto Protocols. Those plans include human trafficking, child kidnapping, torture, and worse.

Thanks to patriots in military intelligence who supported Trump's run for the presidency, he knew well before he won the election that human trafficking – including the abduction of children for really vile purposes – was in fact a global issue. That is why he signed an Executive Order that started the process of putting an end to this despicable trade. We'll get to that, but first, some background.

The Deep State/Cabal has been involved in human trafficking for many decades. At times this has been well known to high level politicians, some of whom have themselves been pedophiles, or engaged in child trafficking as well.

"Crime Against Children"

You may recall that the FBI noted, when investigating the Weiner laptop, that the Clinton Foundation was engaged in "crime against children."

Nothing has come of that so far, but it seems highly likely that when he was campaigning for the presidency, Donald Trump knew about this.

In one debate, candidate Hillary Clinton said we should be glad that Donald Trump was not in charge of the law, to which he responded, "You'd be in jail."

That one line probably did much to ensure his election, and her defeat.

The Clintons, Bill in particular, also got involved in a case of child smuggling out of Haiti after that devastating 2010 earthquake.

A woman, Laura Silsby, who had previously associated with or communicated with the Clintons was charged with child kidnapping and sentenced to jail in Haiti.

Bill Clinton, who had been appointed as overseer of the billions in donated aid (which disappeared) made a special trip to Haiti, talked to someone in that country's government, and the woman's jail term was substantially reduced.

If memory serves, Silsby's "adoption agency" was run under the banner of being a Baptist enterprise out of Utah.

An independent journalist at coreysdigs.com (https://bit.ly/3dolGjn) has thoroughly researched and written an in-depth article about child trafficking. She (Corey) references the Clinton Foundation, billionaires Richard Branson and George Soros.

The first paragraph reads:- "Bill Clinton was recently in Saint Lucia celebrating the new solar farm that the Clintons were instrumental in erecting. Who knew that the Clintons and Richard Branson were spearheading a renewable energy project across the entire Caribbean known as the 'Ten Island Challenge,' locking in every island, forming a perimeter around all their favorite places, such as Haiti, the Dominican Republic, Jamaica, Aruba, Bahamas, Puerto Rico, Venezuela, Colombia, Kenya, and Tanzania? If one didn't know better, isn't that the route drug traffickers and child traffickers utilize?"

Further on, she writes:- "More questions are raised when looking back to the State Department cover-up of pedophilia that plagued the MSM when Hillary Clinton was Secretary of State. As the New York Post (https://bit.ly/3dtbOEX) CBS, and NBC news reported in June, 2013, they had obtained documents tied to ongoing investigations involving eight cases of alleged misconduct by State Department workers, contractors, and a United States ambassador, all of which occurred during Hillary Clinton's tenure.

An internal Inspector General memo from October 2012 reported the ambassador under investigation 'routinely ditched his protective security detail in order to solicit sexual favors from BOTH prostitutes and minor CHILDREN.' The report also states that a high-ranking official at the State Department directed investigators to 'cease the investigations'. Hard to swallow?"

Corey suggests the purpose of the whole endeavor was to create a chain of hotels and restaurants on the islands under the guise of promoting tourism. However, it would also be possible for pedophiles to use fetish-related code words when booking rooms or ordering meals so they could be supplied with enslaved children according to their horrible preferences.

All of the above was going on under Hillary Clinton's watch as Secretary of State, and while Obama was president.

800,000 Trafficked

As Corey's article points out, it had been known for many years that as many as 800,000 humans were being trafficked across borders every year, 50% of them being minors.

In 2014 the International Labor Organization said "forced labor in the private economy generates $150 billion in illegal profits per year, three times more than previously estimated." And that does not include anything about the money made off those who are enslaved in the sex and pedophilia trades; and certainly nothing at all about the victims whose lives are given over to those who practice Satanic rituals.

By now it should be clear that President Trump had every reason to immediately take action and then create and sign an Executive Order to combat this vile industry.

While that Executive Order would specifically relate to the global issue of human trafficking and money laundering, he must surely have been planning to crack down on the sex trade in America as well, especially since pedophilia had been rampant but largely ignored by US government agencies for many years.

Since leaving office Obama has said his administration was free of scandal – perhaps forgetting about the sale of guns to Mexican cartels resulting in the killing of two border patrol agents. Or the IRS going after his political opponents. Or the fact that he jailed a reporter.

A further contradiction to that claim, or at least something that raises many searching questions, would be the release by Wikileaks (https://bit.ly/3drIsqu) of a number of emails from the Stratfor "global intelligence" company.

One among three of those emails said "Get Ready For Chicago Hot Dog Friday." It stated that Obama had spent $65,000 flying pizza and hot dogs from Chicago to the White House for a Friday night party.

The email sequence reads:-
From: Don Kuykendall [mailto: kuykendall@stratfor.com]
Sent: Thursday, May 14, 2009 1:59 PM
To: 'stratforaustin'
Subject: Get ready for "Chicago Hot Dog Friday"
"To celebrate all you hot dogs out there. Aaric, you can participate as
well!"

From: Fred Burton [mailto: burton@stratfor.com]
Sent: Thursday, May 14, 2009 2:39 PM
To: 'Don Kuykendall'
Cc: 'Aaric Eisenstein'; 'Darryl O'Connor'; 'Copeland Susan'
Subject: RE: Get ready for "Chicago Hot Dog Friday"
"I think Obama spent about $65,000 of the tax-payers money flying in
pizza/dogs from Chicago for a private party at the White House not long ago, assume we are using the same channels?"

RE: Get ready for "Chicago Hot Dog Friday"
"If we get the same 'waitresses,' I'm all for it!!!"
Aaric S. Eisenstein
"What are we really talking about here? 'Pizza?' 'Hot Dogs?' 'Waitresses?'"

The FBI website has a page or two (https://bit.ly/3dnT8Xh)

dedicated to the subject of analyzing criminal codes and cyphers, "both of which are used extensively by criminals to conceal clandestine records, conversations and writings."

The FBI also has a list of known pedophile symbols, such as a small blue spiral shaped symbol surrounded by a larger triangle. The small triangle represents a boy, the large one represents an adult man. The symbol represents a "boy lover." There's another symbol for little boys" These symbols are replicated in jewelry such as rings, ear rings and necklaces.

Although the FBI has been cracking down on pedophiles and child traffickers using those symbols on the Internet, the FBI site does not appear to include code words used by these deviants. That's probably a very wise move. Why let your potential targets know what you know about their codes?

A search on "pedophile code words" once again takes us to newspunch.com (https://bit.ly/2yDXmLA) and a story about Wikileaks having released emails attributed to John Podesta, chairman of Hillary Clinton's 2016 campaign. They "incongruously refer to food items such as pasta, cheese pizza, ice cream – which 4chan users say is a code language used by child sex ring participants." (https://bit.ly/3bdy7gD).
"hotdog" = boy
"pizza" = girl
"cheese" = little girl
"pasta" = little boy
"ice cream" = male prostitute
"walnut" = person of colour
"map" = semen
"sauce" = orgy

From that list, we may suspect that the "Hot Dogs" and "Pizza" that were flown from Chicago to the White House were young boys and girls. The subject has certainly received a lot of attention, and investigation, on at least one Twitter thread (https://bit.ly/2L9me0s). Or we can just choose to believe that it was only hot dogs and pizza.

The real evidence that President Trump is serious about destroying these drug and human trafficking operations, comes from a comparison of the numbers of sex trafficking arrests made under his predecessor Obama over a six-year period, and the first two years of the Trump presidency.

Under Obama, starting with only 300 sex trafficking arrests in 2010, a total of 9242 such arrests were made in the six years to 2016.

In came President Trump. His first year, 2017, saw 3213 arrests, followed by 5987 in 2018 to yield a total of 9200 in his first two years in office, compared to 9242 in the previous six years under Obama.

The crackdown on child pornography and pedophiles continues to take such perverts off the streets and into prison. Arrests are being reported by the score throughout the country. Another search finds the following:- February 7 2020 – Stanislaus County, Calif. — "A sweeping, statewide sex trafficking sting led to dozens of arrests in Stanislaus County and hundreds across California, law enforcement officials confirmed Thursday afternoon." (https://bit.ly/2A7BpVQ).

February 18 2020 – HOUSTON - "More than 30 people were arrested as part of an undercover human trafficking operation in eastern Harris County last month." (https://bit.ly/3dnP0Xh).

For more details, you may wish to check out a site started by a concerned Qanon. QMAP: Human trafficking arrests (https://bit.ly/2WcJ0Lp) or https://qmap.pub/kids

Prayer Wall

The site has a prayer wall, and covers subjects such as global themes, players, notable deaths, videos, resignations (there have been hundreds among politicians and corporations - though it would be wrong to even think they were all related to sex trafficking).

The site also covers Executive Orders, sealed cases, and human trafficking. At least up to October 19 2019 it offers a searchable list of human trafficking arrests reported in the news, including illegal immigrants found locked in semi-trailers at the southern border.

Once again, referring back to the Toronto Protocols, it becomes more and more obvious that "they" were making truly significant strides in their efforts to destroy families, at any cost.

Over time, they saw the rewards for their manipulation of society bear fruit in the form of a loss of morality thanks to the work of the media and Hollywood (Disney etc) focusing on errant sexual proclivities, surreptitiously and sometimes openly championing different sexual orientations as "normal."

What adults do behind closed doors is their private business, but if it involves innocent children who should be the most protected people on the planet, that's a whole different story.

Yet, thanks again to the insidious protocols, we now have confused parents seriously believing they should let their infant children decide for themselves what sex they are, while other adults – including even priests and others in the religious community – openly tout their mantra that "child love" and pedophilia should be accepted as normal.

It isn't. Not by any stretch of the imagination.

EXECUTIVE ORDER 138128

Honestly, there are days when I look out at the world, and all I see is a replay of the days of Sodom and Gomorrah.

Hopefully, where Sodom and Gomorrah disappeared in a cloud of radioactive dust (or whatever it was that wiped them out) there is still hope that this civilization, which on the whole has ceased to evolve, just might do the phoenix thing and rise from the ashes.

And that is surely a fitting metaphor for a country that this president has been in a sense resurrecting since Day One of his inauguration – a country that was being burned to the ground by Globalists, coup plotters, and traitors who would do anything to foil his sworn intention to Make America Great Again.

One step in that direction was his signing of Executive Order 138128.

With little attention from the media, on December 20 2017 he signed that Executive Order "Blocking the Property of Persons Involved in Serious Human Rights Abuse or Corruption" (https://bit.ly/2yzYqAh).

It opens as follows:- "By the authority vested in me as President by the Constitution and the laws of the United States of America ... I, Donald J Trump, President of the United States of America, find that the prevalence and severity of human rights abuse and corruption that have their source, in whole or in substantial part, outside the United States, such as those committed or directed by persons listed in the Annex to this order, have reached such scope and gravity that they threaten the stability of international political and economic systems.

"Human rights abuse and corruption undermine the values that form an essential foundation of stable, secure, and functioning societies; have devastating impacts on individuals; weaken democratic institutions; degrade the rule of law; perpetuate violent conflicts; facilitate the activities of dangerous persons; and undermine economic markets. The United States seeks to impose tangible and significant consequences on those who commit serious human rights abuse or engage in corruption, as well as to protect the financial system of the United States from abuse by these same persons.

"I therefore determine that serious human rights abuse and corruption around the world constitute an unusual and extraordinary threat to the national security, foreign policy, and economy of the United States, and I hereby declare a national emergency to deal with that threat.

"I hereby determine and order:" ... and then it goes into legalese which, in my limited understanding of such terms, means something like ....
- anybody involved in any way in any of the above will have their property blocked. (There's a list of names attached to the order.)
- Corrupt government officials are on notice.
- Money laundering (my term) by way of donations is prohibited.
- No prior notice will be given to anyone if their property is to be seized.

CLINTON CONNECTION?

Among the 13 people from various countries named in the annex to that Executive Order was a certain Goulnora Islamovna Karimova of Uzbekistan.

The name seemed to ring a bell, so I checked my images file under "Clinton." Why? Because memory was telling me I had a picture of a certain Bill Clinton alongside a woman from Uzbekistan.

At the time I used that image I was writing an article and later made a video about the Clinton Foundation and Bill Clinton's role in the disappearance of billions of dollars donated by people around the world to help the many victims of the massive 2010 Haiti earthquake.

The search paid off. I found an image of Bill Clinton and a woman named Karimova, but had to ask myself, "is she the Karimova mentioned in the EO that says a corrupt person's assets can be frozen?"

Back to duckduckgo and more checking on keywords "karimova uzbekistan."

What a surprise. Eurasianet ran a story on February 26 2020 saying "The imprisoned daughter of Uzbekistan's late president has said in a statement that she is prepared to relinquish claims to $686 million held in frozen Swiss bank accounts in exchange for clemency in her case." (https://bit.ly/2WyhE1b)

It doesn't say who froze those Swiss accounts, but her offer to pay her way out of her predicament didn't do her any good at all. Just three weeks later, from The Times in London, on March 18 2020:- "The daughter of Uzbekistan's late dictator was today jailed for 13 years after a court found her guilty of heading a crime gang involved in extortion, fraud and money laundering." (https://bit.ly/3cbOsnn)

Are you wondering why Bill Clinton would be associating with a fraudster, the leader of a crime gang involved in extortion, fraud and money laundering? I did. Was it just a case of birds of a feather flocking together? Were they partners in crime? Like many others, I was also wondering when the hammer will come down on the Globalist Clintons.

That aside, the point here is that President Trump's Executive Order of 2017 has clearly had consequences. While there is no mention in any of these reports about human trafficking, it's reasonable to assume that such charges would be much harder to prove than those related to money laundering; money transactions can be tracked, bank accounts can be frozen, whereas human smugglers and traffickers and child violaters would probably have to be caught in the act in order to make a watertight case.

Nevertheless, freezing their money and property assets, and imprisoning some, as in this case, effectively takes them out of the international human trafficking gangland.

As for the national plague of child abuse pornography and human trafficking in the US, President Trump moved on that as well with another Executive Order.

US TRAFFICKING

On January 31 2020 President Trump signed the "Executive Order on Combating Human Trafficking and Online Child Exploitation in the United States."

"Section 1. Policy.
"Human trafficking is a form of modern slavery. Throughout the United States and around the world, human trafficking tears apart communities, fuels criminal activity, and threatens the national security of the United States. It is estimated that millions of individuals are trafficked around the world each year — including into and within the United States.

"As the United States continues to lead the global fight against human trafficking, we must remain relentless in resolving to eradicate it in our cities, suburbs, rural communities, tribal lands, and on our transportation networks. Human trafficking in the United States takes many forms and can involve exploitation of both adults and children for labor and sex.

"Twenty-first century technology and the proliferation of the internet and mobile devices have helped facilitate the crime of child sex trafficking and other forms of child exploitation. Consequently, the number of reports to the National Center for Missing and Exploited Children of online photos and videos of children being sexually abused is at record levels.

"The Federal Government is committed to preventing human trafficking and the online sexual exploitation of children.

Effectively combating these crimes requires a comprehensive and coordinated response to prosecute human traffickers and individuals who sexually exploit children online, to protect and support victims of human trafficking and child exploitation, and to provide prevention education to raise awareness and help lower the incidence of human trafficking and child exploitation into, from, and within the United States.

"To this end, it shall be the policy of the executive branch to prioritize its resources to vigorously prosecute offenders, to assist victims, and to provide prevention education to combat human trafficking and online sexual exploitation of children."

The Order aims to ... "Improve law enforcement's capabilities to detect in real-time the sharing of child sexual abuse material on the internet, including material referred to in Federal law as 'child pornography;'
"Coordinate activities, as appropriate, with the Task Force on Missing and Murdered American Indians and Alaska Natives as established by Executive Order 13898 of November 26, 2019 (Establishing the Task Force on Missing and Murdered American Indians and Alaska Natives)." (https://bit.ly/2SLUh3b)

....

Using the keywords "sex trafficking arrests" yields many results referring to sting operations and arrests throughout the United States.

One in particular, from usatoday.com (https://bit.ly/3ffThNv) authored by Cara Kelly is headlined "13 Sex Trafficking Statistics that Explain the Enormity of the Global Sex Trade."

In a four-minute video on that page we are told "victims live in fear, making convictions hard to get."

We also learn that the slave masters turn their slaves into drug addicts so they can "perform" without conscience. As one interviewee puts it, the profits for the slave owner can amount to thousands of dollars a week.

Kelly writes that "The prominence of illegal parlors and their ties to sex trafficking drew national attention in February with the arrest of New England Patriots owner Robert Kraft and hundreds of other men who police say solicited sex acts in Florida spas. In March, Martin County Sheriff Will Snyder told USA TODAY that the spas involved had "all the trappings of human trafficking."

It is estimated that there are 9000 illicit massage parlors in the US alone; "the vast majority of reported traffic victims are from China" (Fujian Province).

Globally, more than 4 million girls and women are trafficked every year; 1 in 7 reported runaways in the US in 2018 was likely a victim of child sex trafficking; girls in foster care are particularly vulnerable.

Profits from forced sexual labor are estimated at $99 billion worldwide. In the U.S. profits are estimated at $2.5 billion annually.

Sex trafficking occurs around major sporting events, such as the Super Bowl, and the Kentucky Derby.

"Law enforcement in Florida say without victim participation, prosecution for human trafficking of adult victims is all but impossible."

Kelly writes that "The State Department's Trafficking in Persons Report (https://bit.ly/30yymks) found the Department of Justice opened significantly fewer human trafficking investigations in 2018 compared to 2017, dropping from 783 to 657. It also reported significantly fewer prosecutions: 230, down from 282. Of the prosecutions, 213 were for sex trafficking, down from 266 in 2017."

On the face of it, that suggests that law enforcement is not making progress against those involved in the trafficking trade. Another way to look at it though, is to see the reduction in numbers as an indication that the 783 investigations and 266 prosecutions in 2017 took hundreds of traffickers out of the trade. Logically, this would mean fewer people to investigate and prosecute the following year. Therefore, a downward trend could well be a sign of significant progress indeed.

Unfortunately, "The State Department's 2019 Trafficking in Persons report found that at the state and local level, victims are still being arrested for crimes they're compelled to commit such as commercial sex work, including child victims."

In my opinion, considering the level of corruption being uncovered at the highest levels of the U.S. justice system, that is (to use a cliche) just the tip of the iceberg. Corruption runs deep, and could well include state prosecutors and even judges who have their own guilty secrets to hide. And money to make.

THE RED DAWN – 1985

Not only did Serge Monast reveal what the members of the Cabal had planned in 1967, he also exposed what transpired at a following gathering in 1985.

He called it the Red Dawn Document.

With much of their 1967 program having been successfully implemented, their agenda was to fine tune the elements relating to the collapse of what they termed "Nation States," while ensuring that the United Nations would become the vehicle of international power.

While the term "Nation States" is used throughout the 1985 report, it was particularly important for the Globalists to "capture" the United States, for without full control of America, from the top down, they could not – can not – complete their NWO agenda.

Occult Practices

My personal takeaway from reading the Red Dawn Document can be reduced to a few paragraphs about the purpose of their Globalist project.

They considered it was time to further divide society by introducing occult practices.

They needed to consolidate control of international finance because that would in turn finance their project.

Also required would be greater control of the European Union, NATO, and the United Nations.

The burgeoning development of the computer - financed in part they said by "Mr. de Rothschild" starting in 1956, was to be used entirely to their advantage. (1985 was the beginning of the Computer Age. IBM had introduced the first home computer in 1981).

Recognizing the fact that up till then it was impossible to really control all individuals on the planet, they foresaw the computer and its worldwide use as an answer to their prayers - to Baal or some other Satanic deity no doubt.

They did in fact refer to computers as the "cornerstone" of their ambitions, for computers had no allegiance to any country, could be connected in a vast network, used to replace people, control people, manipulate people, and eventually totally control world commerce right down to the individual's everyday transactions using credit and debit cards. For them, computers were seen as "the ultimate tool."

By establishing a worldwide network, computers would effectively remove the existing sense of personal nationalism; users would gradually see themselves as part of a worldwide community, transcending borders in favor of the belief that they were citizens of a global village.

Meanwhile, the Globalists would use their own experts in computer science to create back doors into every computer, harvesting data that could be used to create algorithms which in turn would exponentially enhance their ability to control people's minds and entire lives.

As just one thread in that international spiderweb, they envisioned using the computer for education purposes, starting children down the path of ignorant subservience at a very young age.

First Virus - Bill Gates

On that subject, it is of interest to note that Bill Gates is credited with having written the first virus code. We should well ask, for what purpose? The answer must be that he was likely creating a prototype virus that would morph into an undetectable application in every computer ever built.

Assuming that is true, which I believe it is, from the very first,"they" have been siphoning everything off the Internet into their own secret super-computers.

Where they are located could be anybody's guess, but whether they're in a building somewhere, or in one of their concealed underground facilities, one might hope that they will at some stage be taken out by something like an earthquake.

With every new iteration of this technology, users have marveled at their convenience while ignoring the fact that these devices have become more and more sophisticated in their gathering (and transmission to the Globalists) of personal data.

No farmer has ever had such intimate control of his flock of sheep. He knows not where they wander, what they eat, who they mate with, where they sleep, what their blood pressure might be, how many times their heart beats in a minute, what their weight is, their past yield of wool, their future potential as an economic unit, and their past provision of multiple young who will in turn become useful moneymakers for the future.

Farmers are also aware that there is such a thing as over-stocking, and from time to time the flock or the herd must be culled. It's a dark analogy but you get the picture I'm sure.

Darker still is the revelation that deliberately engineered wars have eliminated countless numbers of people who as far as "they" were concerned had no value as units of profit - except that, through war, the multinationals they control have made billions if not trillions of dollars, while also enabling the takeover of governments or the installation of those aligned with their cause.

To further their demoralization of youth, they funded the research that led to the introduction of the video, knowing that the games they would produce would further desensitize the millions of players attracted to virtual killing and violence.

The 1985 conference came up with a list if 27 ways to make the world in their image. We have seen the establishment of Free Trade agreements over many years - agreements which President Trump has said more than once have been at the expense of the United States. He has pulled the plug on some of them and negotiated better deals, always saying it is a matter of putting America first.

In a sense we could say the Globalist agenda is being torn apart, not with the contempt that Speaker Pelosi showed when she ripped up her copy of his 2020 State Of The Union address, but with the best interests of America in mind.

No wonder "they" want him out. He is the only thing standing in the way of their plan to put the finishing touches to their New World Order.
As Commander-In-Chief he took other steps to foil them. He announced that America would no longer openly reveal its strategies and intentions in areas of conflict such as Iraq, Syria and Afghanistan.

He immediately beefed up the military and they in turn got on with the job of destroying the ISIS caliphate which had flourished during the term of the previous administration. (Obama himself is on video, recorded as saying as part of a new strategy in the war in Syria, America would be arming and training "ISIL" - which later became known as ISIS.)

Aside from the deaths and injuries among troops on all sides of those conflicts, hundreds of thousands and perhaps millions of civilians have lost their lives. Millions more have become homeless refugees, flooding Europe in an almost endless wave, bringing with them the seeds of destruction of those "nation states" - exactly as predicted and then created by the 1985 gathering.

The result for Europe has been economic destabilization, an increase in racial tensions, and further suppression of citizens' rights by increasingly totalitarian governments. Exactly as planned; but only up to a point.

Masters of Deception

Without going into verbatim detail about that 1985 meeting, we can look back from the present through events we have seen over the past 35 years.

Through the lens of a new awareness of what these Masters of Deception have been up to, we can detect what till now has been the almost invisible fingerprint of an unseen hand that has been pulling the levers of control.

Using the International Monetary Fund (the IMF), the World Bank, and Central banks in all but a very few countries, they have indebted most nation states well beyond their ability to repay. The only collateral associated with those loans would have been a country's natural resources, meaning that at a certain point, their debt could be "forgiven" - in exchange for the Globalist multinationals taking control of as much as one third of a country's remaining wild land and whatever oil and minerals it might contain.

With the help of compliant politicians, including former US presidents, China and other countries became a source of cheap labor and therefore apparently cheap goods for western consumers. For the most part, consumers were lulled into a sense of security because prices did not go up.

What most did not notice was that local production was being downsized and many companies were forced out of business.

There was also a continual increase in unemployment numbers, along with a big reduction in internal revenue because companies that went overseas were no longer subject to taxes in their former country.

Millions Mind-Controlled

Jumping to another subject, have you noticed the way much of the media now has an international reach, such as CNN being available 24/7 in international airports, thereby controlling, as usual, the subject matter that millions are exposed to. Fake News knows no boundaries.

Nor does Fake Entertainment. Again, we can see with 20/20 hindsight, how the crooning of Frank Sinatra and the humor of Dean Martin has devolved into sexually explicit gyrations of the Madonnas and Lady Gagas of the present day - some of them now having as many as 3 million followers on the likes of Twitter.

Who do you think controls the artists themselves, and through them, the minds of those millions of followers? You don't have to be one of millions of underpaid seamstresses in a third world sweat shop to be a slave; you can be anything from a pop star to a movie star, to a CEO or even a politician at any level of the political spectrum.

Truth be told, whether you are aware of it or not, you only have to be yourself to be enslaved in some way. Are we not all enslaved by this current economic system with its fiat money, debit and credit cards, mortgaged houses, financed vehicles, and endless debt?

How long is it since America was a nation of social harmony? How long since demonstration s against government policy (as in the case of protests over the Vietnam war) changed from being the people as a collective willing to unite for a real cause, to demonstrations today that pit citizen against citizen based on (manufactured) gender, racial, or political issues? Has this not at times had concerned observers speaking of the possibility of civil war?

How well the Illuminati has cast its net.

GOD WINS!

President Trump, along with Q and the Qanons, are at the forefront of this battle between the Dark, and the Light, determined to take down those who would undermine and destroy everything genuine Americans stand for.

Fortunately for us, and the world itself, countermeasures are in place.

Often, Qanons post a meme saying "God wins!" This, and the use of Bible versus by Q, run entirely counter to the Illuminati desire to destroy the judeo-Christian underpinnings of American society.

Perhaps as part of that endeavor, we saw former president Obama surrounded by people of Muslim faith, while Hillary Clinton's closest friend, Huma Abedin, has lifetime family ties to the Muslim Brotherhood.

As a matter of policy the brotherhood is dedicated to replacing all forms of Western government with Sharia law. Abedin's inclusion in Hillary Clinton's inner circle has been categorized by Q as infiltration (by the brotherhood presumably) rather than invasion.

The same is true of many appointments throughout government and its agencies. Former CIA Director John Brennan spent many years overseas. He converted to Islam, and speaks some Farsi. He was appointed to the CIA position by fellow Muslim,

Barrack Hussein Obama.

Perhaps, at some level, those terrible Crusades that saw the slaughter of thousands of innocents among Christians and Muslims of the time have never really ended.

Where they used horses and swords and scimitars, today the adversaries use modern weapons, but the results are the same - death and destruction on all sides.

Unfortunately, that serves the Illuminati agenda just fine.

Have Faith

Individually, we have our personal views of religion, God and the Bible, Allah and the Koran, the Bhagavagita, Krishna, Jesus, Mohammad and so many different paths that are followed by millions. Nevertheless, this is no place to question the beliefs of others in any way.

What can be said is that the Cabal/Deep State badly misread the strength of the judeo-Christian ethic in America, and its influence on some in the military and law enforcement, on a number of presidents (Kennedy and Reagan being but two examples) and on still many millions of patriotic Americans.

It may not be the only reason, but that faith surely played a major part in seeing Donald Trump elected, and in the ever-growing support for him and his policies.

Stepping back to the midterm election cycle, it is worth noting Q's Post 2403 of November 4 2018. For the Republicans, it was imperative that they take control of the Senate.

The Post reads:-
"Your Country Needs You.
"Your Vote Matters!
"We, the People.
(At this point, Q inserted a link to a YouTube video featuring many of President Reagan's speeches about America's role as the

world's greatest military power - a power that must be used to ensure peace on Earth. I suggest you now follow that link, pause and reflect, then return to this post and its Bible reference (https://bit.ly/3hiwwtW).
The post continues:-
"The Time is Now.
"Patriots Fight!
"Finally, be strong in the Lord and in his mighty power.

"Put on the full armor of God so that you can take your stand against the devil's schemes. For our struggle is not against flesh and blood, but against the rulers, against the authorities, against the powers of this dark world and against the spiritual forces of evil in the heavenly realms.
"Therefore put on the full armor of God, so that when the day of evil comes, you may be able to stand your ground, and after you have done everything, to stand. Stand firm then, with the belt of truth buckled around your waist, with the breastplate of righteousness in place, and with your feet fitted with the readiness that comes from the gospel of peace.

"In addition to all this, take up the shield of faith, with which you can extinguish all the flaming arrows of the evil one. Take the helmet of salvation and the sword of the Spirit, which is the word of God. And pray in the Spirit on all occasions with all kinds of prayers and requests. With this in mind, be alert and always keep on praying for all the saints." – Ephesians 6:10-18

"We hold these truths to be self-evident, that all men are created equal, that they are endowed by their Creator with certain unalienable Rights, that among these are Life, Liberty and the pursuit of Happiness.

"That to secure these rights, Governments are instituted among Men, deriving their just powers from the consent of the governed, –That whenever any Form of Government becomes destructive of these ends, it is the Right of the People to alter or to abolish it, and to institute new Government, laying its foundation on such principles and organizing its powers in such form, as to them shall seem most likely to effect their Safety and Happiness.

"Prudence, indeed, will dictate that Governments long established should not be changed for light and transient causes; and accordingly all experience hath shewn, that mankind are more disposed to suffer, while evils are sufferable, than to right themselves by abolishing the forms to which they are accustomed.
"But when a long train of abuses and usurpations, pursuing invariably the same Object evinces a design to reduce them under absolute Despotism, it is their right, it is their duty, to throw off such Government, and to provide new Guards for their future security."
– Declaration of Independence
"We Will Do Our Job to Protect the Vote.
"Will You Do Yours?
"Will You Answer the Call?
"WWG1WGA!!!"
Q

Unless these forces of evil, which are embodied in the Illuminati agenda, are defeated, the future is bleak indeed.

They intended to purge those of judeo-Christian persuasion from the military and law enforcement; they schemed to transform the UN peace-keeping forces into a global army; transfer existing military bases to the control of the UN; to introduce surveillance cameras and drones to spy on and control the populace; continue control of the media; create data bases on every individual on the planet; gain total control of all firearms on the planet (using "crazy shooters" and what that implies as part of that).

Many times we have seen reports of mass murders by crazy shooters, not just in America, but around the world. New Zealand, Australia, Britain, Germany are just a few that come to mind. \

Why would they build such horrific events into their New World Order plan? Because, in a nutshell, without full control of firearms, it would be all but impossible for their plans to succeed.

Keep that in mind - especially if you are an anti-gun advocate. Guns have been used by both men and women from pioneering times to the present day in order to protect their neighbors, themselves, their families and loved ones. Guns were essential in creating this country. We can but hope they will not be needed in order to keep it.

Hopefully, given President Trump's insistence that the Second Amendment (the right to bear arms) will not be repealed, at least under his watch, there will be no outbreak of yet another civil war in this country.

Q may often say "Fight Fight Fight," but I personally interpret that not to mean the use of weapons, but to fight by spreading truth and facts and participating in the electoral process.

"Fighting" can be done by supporting good local candidates in elections, and, of course, by fighting to see President Trump remain in office.

If his opponents can fight as hard as they do to remove him, should his supporters not fight just as hard, in every peaceful way possible, to keep him in the White House?

BLACK HATS - BLACK BUDGETS

While thanks to their political affiliates the Cabal has seen many nation states now having laws on the books that essentially mimic those of Nazi Germany, regulating the (non)possession of firearms, that is just one small aspect of their interlocking subversive activities.

If you recall the shooting down of US pilot Gary Powers while on a spy flight over the Soviet Union in his top secret U2 aircraft, you might also recall that the U2 had been in service for about 20 years - and nobody in the general public knew about it.

The same must be said about mysterious "black budget" programs, some of which are totally and secretly in the service of the Globalists.

To confirm this, you could pick your own keywords and search for such things as "secret space program," or "underground bases" or "Nazis + Antarctica," or "electromagnetic weapons," or "electromagnetic weapons + HAARP."

Such weapons can be used to alter the climate in any given location, thereby controlling food production by creating floods or droughts or unseasonable hotter wetter colder dryer winters and summers - take your pick. Food shortages to the point of famine are therefore controllable.

Earthquakes can be triggered, perhaps right down to determining the size of the 'quake. If we accept that as possible, then was the Haiti earthquake natural or man-made? Was the great Hokkaido 'quake in Japan natural or man-made?

Would it be useful from "their" point of view to create earthquakes in major industrial regions of various countries, thereby helping to ruin their economies?

Or could such technology, in the hands of the "White Hats," be used to demolish certain underground bases and cities - as some social media users have said is happening?

If the Deep State/Cabal has been implementing all the above without the wider public having any clue that it has been happening, how do they expect to continue their campaign of dominance as more and more individuals join the Qanon movement?
The answer is simple. The more people become aware and awake, the less the chances of the Black Hats achieving their goal.

Documents such as the Toronto Protocols are shocking in themselves, but even they do not tell the full story. What we do know, however, is that child slavery (and worse), the ravaging of the Third World, control of the multi-billion-dollar drug industry, racial conflicts, manufactured divisions in society, promotion of pedophilia and abnormal sexuality, control of the immoral entertainment industry, these and more have all combined to bring the world far too close to their dream of a New World Order.

SILENT WEAPONS

The Globalists were in on the ground floor as computers were developed, and the Internet has most certainly served them in their quest for world domination. But only up to a point.

With Q appearing on the Internet in 2017, and the following diligent research by millions of Qanons, we find a link to a document called "Silent Weapons for Quiet Wars, An Introduction Programming Manual."

It was used as the basis for the first known Bilderberg meeting in 1954.

The document was used in full by the late William (Bill) Cooper, author of *Behold a Pale Horse* (1991). Cooper was eventually killed in a shoot-out with cops who purportedly came to arrest him for threatening a complainant with a handgun. He shot one of the cops dead before he himself was killed. The official report does not specify who fired the first shot.

I read the book many years ago, but still clearly recall him writing about being on lookout on a submarine sailing from Seattle down to California. He said he saw a large circular craft rise from the water, disappear into the clouds, then reappear and submerge itself once again in the ocean.

Having had my own encounters and sightings (including directing the documentary, *"Contact Has Begun,"* which is available on my website) I had no reason to question or dismiss Cooper's story about that incident.

Naturally, he was told he should never reveal what he had seen. But he did. And a whole lot more. Both he and Serge Monast paid with their lives.

Copyright law prevents me from using Cooper's work in full, although as far as I know, the document he referred to as having been found in a discarded IBM copy machine, has no copyright attached to it.

Cooper was not the original author, and since the document was published by some obscure (secretive) government department, copyright does not apply.
Therefore, Clause 7 of the Copyright Act allows for use of a limited amount of its contents "for purposes such as criticism, comment, news reporting, teaching... scholarship, or research." These are "not an infringement of copyright."

The introduction to the Internet version by Wes Penre, dated December 14 2003, says in part:- "TOP SECRET: Silent Weapons for Quiet Wars, An introductory Programming Manual," was uncovered quite by accident on July 7th, 1986 when an employee of Boeing Aircraft Co. purchased a surplus IBM copier for scrap parts at a sale, and discovered inside details of a plan, hatched in embryonic days of the Cold War, which called for control of the masses through manipulation of Industry, peoples' pastimes, education and political learning's. It called for a quite (sic) revolution, putting (sic) brother against brother, and diverting the public's attention from what is really going on."

"Control The Whole World.."

The manual goes into detail about how, with the development

and evolution of the computer and the ability to gather reams of social data "those in positions of power strongly suspected that it was possible for them to control the whole world with the push of a button."

It says the Rockefeller Foundation "got in on the ground floor by making a four year grant to Harvard College, funding the Harvard economic research project for the study of the structure of the American economy."

Aware that it was only a matter of time before the general public "would also be able to grasp and upset the cradle of power" through their access to the same computer technology, for the elite the "issue of primary concern, that of dominance, revolved around the subject of the energy sciences."

We - the general public - are accustomed to thinking of energy in forms of oil, perhaps hydro power and electricity from dams, or nuclear energy such as power plants or even nuclear weapons. But according to the Manual, there is also social energy which can be tracked and graphed like a "bookkeeping system" through the study of economics and the use of mathematics. "And the bookkeeper can be king if the public can be kept ignorant of the methodology of the bookkeeping."

The Manual speaks of ensuring that education is of the poorest sort so that ignorance ensures the "inferior class" remains in a form of slavery that "is essential to maintaining some measure of social order, peace, and tranquility for the ruling upper class."

They foresaw the introduction of universal product codes and credit cards which could be used together to gather data right down to the individual person level; such data could then be mathematically assessed and the results used to further control the economy, society, and the production and movement of goods and services.

On reflection, their strategy aimed at controlling the public has been brilliantly effective. Unless countermeasures are taken, and are successful, it could well result in the final adoption of a New World Order, controlled of course by the elite.

Their strategy boils down to keeping the public "undisciplined and ignorant," and "confused, disorganized and distracted with matters of no real importance."
They have largely achieved that goal by ensuring low quality education, "a constant barrage of sex, violence, and wars in the media - especially the TV and newspapers. Giving them 'junk food for thought,' and rewriting history and law."

IRS - Silent Weapon

This brief review of the "Top Secret Document" hardly scratches the surface of its contents. It is definitely an important stop on your research journey. As a final mention, which explains why one of life's only certainties is taxes, the Manual reveals that the Internal Revenue Service (IRS) is an essential component of their silent weaponry.

"Much information is made available to silent weapons systems programers through the Internal Revenue Service. This information consists of the enforced delivery of well organized data submitted by slave labor provided by taxpayers and employers. When the government is able to collect tax and seize private property without just compensation, it is an indication that the public is ripe for surrender and is consenting to enslavement and legal encroachment. A good indicator of harvest time is the number of public citizens who pay income tax despite an obvious lack of reciprocal or honest service from government."

To further your research the full document is available at this link (https://bit.ly/3ccUAeN).

ROCKEFELLER SCENARIOS

In 2010 the Rockefeller Foundation produced a report that was focused on future scenarios.

Its opening graphic is a world map with every continent depicted in the form of ones and zeros, similar to what you might have seen in movies like The Matrix series where the ones and zeros cascade down a screen.

It is a symbol of today's high technology, which as we know, can be used for both good and bad purposes.

The title of the report is "Scenarios for the Future of Technology and International Development."
Before we go there, some research is in order.

Briefly, who are the Rockefellers? They are an American dynasty, similar to the Rothschild family dynasty of Europe.

They are unabashed Globalists. The Rockefellers donated $8 million in 1946 with which 16 acres of land in New York was purchased for the United Nations headquarters.

To a thinking person, the very name, "United Nations," is an in-your-face clue as to their ultimate goal – the New World Order, which means a world united under a global government, a one world religion, and the end of sovereign states and constitutions such as that of the United States of America.

Rockefeller Quotes

"David Rockefeller (June 12, 1915 – March 20, 2017) was an American banker who served as chairman and chief executive of Chase Manhattan Corporation. He was the oldest living member of the third generation of the Rockefeller family, and family patriarch from August 2004 until his death in March 2017." - Wikipedia. (https://bit.ly/2A7oOSw)

"Some even believe we are part of a secret cabal working against the best interests of the United States, characterizing my family and me as internationalists and of conspiring with others around the world to build a more integrated global political and economic structure, one world, if you will. If that's the charge, I stand guilty, and am proud of it." - *David Rockefeller.*

"The end goal is to get everybody chipped, to control the whole society, to have the bankers and the elite people control the world " - Nick Rockefeller in his Aaron Russo interview (https://bit.ly/2WcdQnu)

"Whatever the price of the Chinese Revolution, it has obviously succeeded not only in producing a more efficient and dedicated administration, but also in fostering high morale and community of purpose. The social experiment of China under Chairman Mao's leadership is one of the most important and successful in human history." - *David Rockefeller.*

"We are grateful to the Washington Post, the New York Times, Time Magazine and other great publications whose directors have attended our meetings and respected their promises of discretion for almost 40 years.....It would have been impossible for us to develop our plan for the world if we had been subjected to the lights of publicity during those years." - *David Rockefeller.*

"The supranational sovereignty of an intellectual elite and world bankers is surely preferable to the national autodetermination practiced in past centuries" - *David Rockefeller*

"We are on the verge of a global transformation. All we need is the right major crisis and the nations will accept the New World Order." - David Rockefeller speaking at a United Nations Business Conference, Sept. 14 1994.

Obfuscation

You might also select some search words of your own to investigate how the Rockefellers have influenced the role of doctors and the pharmaceutical industry since at least 1890, but for now, we should focus on the report the foundation published in 2010, and the scenarios it envisaged. It runs to 51 pages, from which we will excerpt the most interesting subject matter.

Please keep in mind that reports such as this are crafted by specialists in obfuscation. They use language that can sound wonderful and authoritative and caring for humanity, telling the truth, but not necessarily the whole truth. They deliberately and inevitably highlight the plight of the poor. They are specialists in manipulating human emotions, fear being the easiest to both create and to use to their advantage.

In harping on the poor and the starving and the underprivileged and the undeveloped third world countries while claiming to do good works for the poor, they know most people will feel a subconscious fear of being poor and hungry and underprivileged - or they will be sympathetic to the do-good concept and ask no questions.

However, such honeyed words can sometimes give you a feeling in the pit of your stomach that "there's something too saccharine about this." And you'd be right. Nevertheless, it works for them.

In this report, they constantly stress their role as a philanthropic organization. That repetition works by way of convincing the masses that they really do really care, while at the same time they are actually telegraphing what they have in store for the future. In this case, a decade ago they were right into "scenario planning."

You can download the full report from this link (https://bit.ly/2TOVIhE).

Creepy Scenario

Perhaps the creepiest of its four projected future scenarios was one involving a pandemic.

On the face of it, the scenarios seem to be simply hypothetical. But are they? What if reports such as this are actually a code for other globalists and their legion of puppets in politics, industry, commerce and science to literally take note of and work toward creating? Just sayin'. But just sayin' because this report, while purporting to present fictional future scenarios, starts with one that is eerily prescient.

It's about a fictional, I repeat, fictional, 2012 future in which a "pandemic that the world had been anticipating for years finally hit. Unlike 2009's H1N1, this new influenza strain—originating from wild geese—was extremely virulent and deadly."

If you have downloaded the full report, you will see that it addresses "the future of globalization," expects population growth to "put pressure on energy food and water resources," claims that scenarios "can be not just envisioned *but also actualized*," speaks about the future and "perhaps most importantly ... *how we can help to create it*."

It may not seem significant, but it probably is - the scenarios they came up with assumed an end date of 2030, although within that 40-year time frame they portrayed four "very different futures."

The first of these was titled LOCK STEP: "A world of tighter top-down government control and more authoritarian leadership, with limited innovation and growing citizen pushback."

The report does ask you to "Please keep in mind that the scenarios in this report are stories, not forecasts, and the plausibility of a scenario does not hinge on the occurrence of any particular detail."

Why do I have a gut feeling that that statement was deliberately inserted as a fallback option so they could claim it was "just a coincidence" when one of their scenarios actually occurred - such as the pandemic they used as the basis for their LOCK STEP scenario?

It reads like this:- "In 2012, the pandemic that the world had been anticipating for years finally hit. Unlike 2009's H1N1, this new influenza strain — originating from wild geese — was extremely virulent and deadly.

"Even the most pandemic-prepared nations were quickly overwhelmed when the virus streaked around the world, infecting nearly 20 percent of the global population and killing 8 million in just seven months, the majority of them healthy young adults.

"The pandemic also had a deadly effect on economies: international mobility of both people and goods screeched to a halt, debilitating industries like tourism and breaking global supply chains. Even locally, normally bustling shops and office buildings sat empty for months, devoid of both employees and customers."

It goes on to say that under that "scenario" authorities around the world imposed multiple restrictions and rules, right down to the wearing of face masks and body temperature checks.

They foresaw the introduction of "biometric IDs" with citizens willingly giving up sovereignty in exchange for safety and stability.

To close the "Lock Step" scenario, the report suggests some likely future headlines, such as "Quarantine restricts in-person contact; cellular networks overloaded (2013)", and "Intercontinental trade hit by strict pathogen controls (2015)" and "Italy addresses 'immigrant caregiver gap with Robots (2017)."

It then goes into how philanthropy might be affected under that scenario. It says "Larger philanthropies will retain an outsized share of influence" which brings to mind the current wall-to-wall media coverage of the Bill Gates Foundation and his incessant and strident calls for every person on the planet to be vaccinated, with a vaccine developed by his associates of course. Imagine that! Bill Gates, by the way, has frequently said the planet is overpopulated.

On the technology side, under that Lock Step scenario, the report says we might see .scanners becoming the norm at airports and other public areas to "detect abnormal behavior that may indicate 'antisocial intent,' new ways to detect communicable diseases which would become a "prerequisite for release from a hospital or prison, successfully slowing the spread of many diseases."

Oddly enough, they also foresaw (theoretically) governments policing Internet traffic (which China certainly does) "but these efforts nevertheless fracture the World Wide Web."

The other three scenarios promote global warming as a major disaster requiring "highly coordinated worldwide strategies for addressing such urgent issues," plus a "functioning global cap and trade system," centralized global oversight and governance structures,as a consequence of which "nation-states lost some of their power and importance as global architecture strengthened," and *"international oversight entities like the UN took on new levels of authority."*

The fly in the ointment as far as the UN taking on more authority goes, is that President Trump has stopped funding the World Health Organization, and we might suspect that it won't be long before the United States withdraws completely from the UN.

Q GOES GLOBAL

Because of the advent of social media, and no thanks at all to the legacy fake news media, the influence of Q's Internet posts and the associated Great Awakening is gathering steam not only in America, but around the Globe.

As evidence of the growth of the Qanon phenomenon, back on September 19 2018 in Post 2224 Q cryptically asked for confirmation about a system resource upgrade, saying "Tracking 330,000 ips which is causing extreme lag." That's 330,000 individual computers being used to access Q's posts by 330,000 Qanons. Some now say the number has grown to as many as 3,000,000.

By now, it may be many more because on June 5 2020, in Post 4426, Q wrote:- Important to understand.
MSDNC [+social media] projection we are the minority is false.
WE ARE THE MAJORITY AND GROWING EVERY SECOND OF THE DAY.
MSDNC [+social media] projection we are divided is false.
WE ARE UNITED AND ONLY GETTING STRONGER.
People are awake and see what is happening.
Patriots have no skin color.
Humanity is good.
Q
(MSDNC presumably refers to the Mainstream Media as an arm of the Democratic National Committee, hence MSDNC).

I have seen photographs and videos of people wearing Q clothing or carrying Q-related signs from Japan, Hong Kong, Canada, the Netherlands and the UK, and have received comments on my YouTube channel from people in Australia, New Zealand, Britain, Mexico, and other countries as well.

In "waking up" they have become aware that "something's not right" and they're starting to rebel against what we might call their (our) overlords.

These overlords, especially within governments around the world, are the puppets whose strings are pulled by those responsible for the Toronto Protocols, and before that, the strategies developed by the Bilderbergers, and before that, the coalition of as many as 13 families, such as the Rothschilds and Rockefellers.

Maybe to the average person it sounds preposterous, but "they" really have been working diligently, subversively, and in many cases treasonously, to control the whole planet.
That's why they fear this Great Awakening and will fight tooth and nail to survive and realize their dream – which is a nightmare for us.

However, while they do number in the thousands, what can they do against an entire nation, or a world, of awakened and pissed off people?

The French Connection

Let's take France as an example. The Deep State is well aware that Q and his almost 4000 posts are an existential threat to their existence.

The worldwide burgeoning awareness of their activities and the ongoing protests in France are examples of people becoming more and more aware. That's not to say they are all Qanons by any means. But they are certainly all pissed off.

On Thursday January 23 2020 Q dropped Post 3792.
It reads:-Absolutely Massive Crowds out on the Streets of France Against Macron Tonight (https://bit.ly/3dizlse)
Q!!Hs1Jq13jV623 Jan 2020 – 3:18:00 PM (https://bit.ly/2YOaLeG)
Remember when the FAKE NEWS MEDIA told you this was all in relation to a gas tax over a year ago?
Sheep no more!
The Great Awakening!
Q

MACRON – GLOBALIST

In the 30 years I have lived in America I have seen first hand how the media operates here. In a word, and I hope it's the right one, it is geocentric.

It is totally US-focused. It is obsessed with politics and politicians. Obsessed with narratives about race, the rantings and ravings of "stars" whether that is in sports or from tinsel town Hollywood, and utterly bereft of a world view.

Why is that?

It is because they are an adjunct of the Cabal. They do not want their viewers listeners or readers to really think for themselves. That is why they seldom if ever run anything but domestic news (unless it might be anti-Trump in some way).

They ignore protests that have been going on in France for over a year. Why? Because you might start thinking that those protests are legitimate grievances against an authoritarian president who loves the elite and has spent a lifetime helping them in their New World Order quest.

You might then start wondering whether or not some of your own politicians are not really who they pretend to be.

But perhaps the main reason they ignored the protests in France was that some of them were wearing vests with the letter Q on them, or carrying Q-related placards.

A Globalist Puppy?

France's president, Emmanuel Jean-Michel Frederic Macron (Macron for short), was born in 1977, 10 years after the Toronto Protocols were enumerated.

At the age of 14 (some say 15 to make the event correspond to the age of consent in France) he was seduced by his school teacher, some 21 years his senior, beginning a relationship that has lasted to this day.

Whether he sees himself as one or not, as puppets go, Macron has proven to be a very useful puppy for the Globalists. Depending how you interpret his bio in Wikipedia (https://bit.ly/3foyeZY), you could say he has the perfect Globalist pedigree.

With a Masters Degree in public affairs he became a senior civil servant in the Inspectorate General of Finances, then moved on to investment banking with Rothschild and Co. (The history of the Rothschilds and their control of empires, especially from the time of Napoleon, is the subject of my first book, *President Trump and the New World Order.*)

From there, he was appointed a deputy secretary general by President Hollande in 2012, and two years later became Minister of the Economy and Industry.
Macron was a Socialist from at least the age of 24, but in his ministerial role he proposed and backed big-business-friendly legislation.

This is where it gets really interesting. In a matter of just two years, he founded his own political party, campaigned, and became president of a country of 67 million people. All in about 24 months. How did he do it?

It is impossible to believe that he single-handedly mounted a campaign that would take him to the presidency. His ascension required a lot of help and a well-oiled strategy. So in 2015 he disavowed socialism and started his own "independent" political movement, En Marche.

It would be no surprise to awakened Qanons who know how the US media is 90% owned and controlled by the Deep State, to learn that the French media immediately fell into lockstep with his campaign.

At the age of 39, on May 14 2017, Macron became the youngest president in French history.
Do you know any 39-year-old that you would trust with such a role?

From Wikipedia:- "Many foreign politicians voiced support for Macron in his bid against right-wing populist candidate Marine Le Pen, including European Commission President Jean-Claude Juncker, German Chancellor Angela Merkel, and former US President Barack Obama."

Ms Marine Le Pen would, I believe, be best described in US political party terms as a right winger; an anti-Globalist if you will. As for Junckers from the EU, Merkel of Germany, and Obama from the US – it's ironic that their voiced support for Macron was never tagged as foreign interference in the French election. All of them are Globalists.

Oddly enough however, two days before the election of May 7 2017, nine gigabytes of Macron's emails related to his election campaign somehow found their way on to the Internet, and were eventually released by Wikileaks.

Macron accused Russia of political interference.

Sound familiar?

What seems to be a logical deduction from the above truncated research, is that the secret powers achieved in France what they failed to achieve in the United States; a leader who would continue to enrich the rich by enacting favorable legislation for them (he scrapped the wealth tax) while continuing to fleece the sheep.

And, like Obama had done during his presidency, Macron weakened the military by cutting their budget by 850 million Euros, leading to the immediate resignation of the Chief of the General Staff of the armies after a confrontation with Macron.

France has major issues with the influx of thousands of Muslim refugees, and its economy is anything but robust.

In February 2020 President Trump was asked by a French reporter why the US economy was doing so much better than that of France. She asked "what's the secret?"

His reply was simple:- "Perhaps we have a better president than you do."

YELLOW VESTS

Events in France and elsewhere in Europe, and the exit of the UK from the EU over the past couple of years are also a good indication that the Great Awakening is happening globally.

In the US, House Speaker Nancy Pelosi may have ripped up her copy of President Trump's State of the Union speech, but here and elsewhere, it looks like ordinary citizens, including many who have probably never heard of Q or Qanon, are starting to rip up the Illuminati playbook.

One thing France's President Macron did, and it backfired big time, was to plan to introduce a fuel tax starting in January 2019.

Diesel, which cost the equivalent of about $6.50 a gallon at the time, was to go up by several cents.

Macron, like his Globalist peers around the world, used the argument that this would reduce the use of that fuel, and thus help abate global warming (a Globalist scam in itself). Well, tell that to a farmer who is already struggling to make ends meet, and what do you get? Hundreds of tractors heading toward Paris, many of their drivers wearing yellow vests – vests which all drivers are required to have in their vehicle in case of need in an emergency.

And thus the "Yellow Vest" movement was born.

Macron backed down and the price rise did not go into effect. Meanwhile, the US media was telling us the protests were entirely over that proposed fuel price rise.

If so, why have those rallies and protests continued right through into 2020, with no sign of them getting smaller? Because France, since the election of their current president, has devolved into turmoil because their president is a Globalist. A quick search for "Q in France" and "images" soon leads to pictures of Yellow Vest protesters and then an article in thenational.ae (https://bit.ly/3dlHwnN).

We find that despite the deployment of 8000 police in Paris when the first protests began in December 2018, and despite the government not going ahead with the fuel tax, the Yellow Vest (gilets jaunes) demonstrations have spread to many French cities.

They're happening every weekend. Thousands have been arrested in confrontations with police using armored vehicles and teargas, but the demonstrations continue to this day.

Literally hundreds of thousands of people are saying they have had enough of the current government, in particular Macron himself, who they call an arrogant "president of the rich."

Macron started his five-year term with a 62% approval rating. Just 18 months later, that was down to 25%. (In America, impeach President Trump, and his ratings go up.)

Among the grievances of the Yellow Vest protesters, though it is very unlikely to be reported by traditional media, is the influx of Muslim refugees. They have created neighborhoods in Paris which the police now avoid – or so it is said on the Internet.

In Britain too there is concern that Muslim refugees, some of whom have attacked and killed innocent people, will eventually turn London into "Londonistan" under Sharia law.

The Muslim Brotherhood is also very active in America, including in politics where a number of Muslims were appointed to various close positions by Obama, and obtained seats in Congress. Their goal is to scrap the Constitution, the rule of law as it stands, and turn America into a Muslim nation under Sharia law.

MIND CONTROL

Seen from the perspective of the Toronto Protocols, with Macron we have a willing and ambitious individual connected to the Rothschilds now in power in France, thanks in no small part to the Illuminati's control of the media.

However, there may be much more to the media's role than that, especially if one is somewhat awake to how the Globalists have operated. Note also that the media is more than just the Fake News componenet. Media includes endless advertising, innumerable films, videos, magazines, radio shows and live entertainment.

We learned from the Toronto Protocols that "they" planned, then aided and abetted the rise of Communism in Russia. Similarly, they used Hitler, hoping for that "thousand year Reich."

Stepping back a bit, and as detailed in my book *President Trump and the New World Order,* prior to America's entry into World War One, which they had planned in advance, they were involved in the sinking of the Lusitania, as a result of which President Woodrow Wilson eventually had America engaged in that war.

In such cases, and there are many others, the loss of life eventually ran into millions upon millions.

As psychopathic and evil as they are, while presenting themselves as having our best interests at heart, these people are nevertheless master psychologists.

They have long understood how to manipulate people, and entire nations. Where mind control projects might use trauma to create multiple personalities in one of their individual "assets,"(think of the Bourne series of movies, or the book *Trance-formation of America* by Cathy O'Brien) the same principle can be applied to an entire nation.

Shock people badly enough, such as with the Twin Towers attack of 9/11, and they will quickly accept any relief that is offered by the powers that be.

In America 911 saw the beginning of the endless "war on terror," and the introduction of the so-called Patriot Act, a cunning misnomer if ever there was one. It was an Act which reduced individual freedoms in exchange for "more security."

As a consequence we now have the Department of Homeland Security, the frisking of grandmothers and children at airports (at least one TSA airport employee has been caught on an iPhone and posted on Facebook, appearing to fondle a young boy's crotch) and never a terrorist found at an airport in about 20 years.
The Illuminati have found many ways to control nations, politicians, societies and individuals.

By analogy, if you are a parent who must control your children, you can use various forms of discipline. In the days before it was "child abuse" which can see you being reported by your children to Child Protective Services, discipline could certainly be harsh, with some parents quite out of control in dealing with their children.

However, the truly vast majority, back then, must surely have done their parenting with love, even if at times it was tough love requiring a trip to the woodshed. The point being, a small trauma like a whack on the butt with Dad's leather belt because of some unacceptable word or behavior, was enough to make a kid change his mind and thus change his behavior.

Ideally, the child would grow up knowing respect for his/her elders and for his/her peers, because for the most part they lived in good families, had their ups and downs, but adhered to good family values that they in turn would pass on to the next generation.

Subliminal Programming

The Cabal however has perfected mind control on a grand scale.

Their techniques do not however always require some super-traumatic event such as 911 which affects an entire society. Aside from dumbing down people through the poorest of educations (which by the way are controlled right up to PhD level) mind controlling technologies, such as subliminal images in magazine photographs and on television have long been used – not to mention the use of deviant pedophile symbols in movies such as *The Lion King* by Disney.

The word "sex" and artful representations of male and female anatomies are carefully crafted into many images, and the magazine industry has even gone so far as to include libido-enhancing scents in their glossy editions.

Surely all of that is evidence that Big Business is doing what was spelled out in those Toronto protocols?

Mass mind control, to the point of influencing an entire society over a span of several generations, is what we're talking about.

The quote "give me a child until he is seven and I will give you the man," has been attributed to both Aristotle and the Catholic Order of Jesuits. Either way, it serves to illustrate the fact that the mind of a child is open to being influenced permanently by what it is taught or learns from its environment.

Children of Catholic parents generally become Catholics, Muslims grow up to adhere to that religion, and whatever is taught in the education system plays a major part in the child's adult future.

Understanding that, the crafters of the Protocols knew full well that by subtly changing a variety of elements within society, they would eventually reach their goal of creating a society divided against itself.

Sadly, but realistically, is that not the case in America right now?

The protocols speak about fracturing and even destroying the traditional family and its family values. They also presaged a world in which coming generations would be "sexually liberated," self-interested, and devoid of any feeling of family unity, local community or national pride.

With their agents such as George Soros stirring the pot wherever he goes, funding groups like Antifa and Black Lives Matter in America and donating thousands if not millions of dollars to help certain people get elected, one could say they have all but completely succeeded.

Such was the state of the nation, and much of the world, when "#OrangeManBad" took office.

During his election campaign, some were saying the Ship of State was in serious danger. If they were thinking of what might happen if Hillary Clinton was elected, they were right. But others believed, or said they believed, that the ship would be in very serious danger with Trump at the helm.

Well, he did become the skipper, and he has been sailing stormy waters ever since.

By 2020, having turned the ship around despite endless attacks by his livid opponents, President Trump had really begun to "Make America Great Again."

He did that in no small part through his internal policies, tax cuts and help for Veterans, but also because he personally took on the task of letting world leaders know that the days of ripping off America were over – which in essence is what he said in his first speech to world leaders at the United Nations.

THE NEW SHERIFF

Unbeknownst to most of us, the world, and America in particular, was on a downhill slope when Donald Trump beat the Globalists' acolyte Hillary Clinton and became President of the United States.

Q has often said "they never thought she would lose." But she did. And despite her excuses ever since, she lost, and that's what happened.

Those who have escaped the headlock of the mainstream media, which insists on running hundreds of anti-Qanon articles, and who have been willing to explore the many posts dropped by Q, have good reason to believe that President Trump is well aware of what the Globalists and their puppet politicians have been up to.

Hence the term "Drain the Swamp."

Thanks to Q, and the research and digging by countless Qanons, it is clear now that President Trump was well aware of the Globalists and their agenda even before he opted to run for the presidency.

Knowing that, we can see his first address to the United Nations in a very different light.

Confronting him were the leaders of many world governments, the majority of whom we can surmise were in one way or another part of the Globalist game-plan.

Trying to be fair, it should be said, perhaps repeatedly, that some if not all of them have been compromised (blackmailed?) into going along with that agenda. How else could the Illuminati plan have come so close to success, if not through the co-operation of the politicians they needed to get it done?

For many in the political realm, even down to the lowest level of governance, the sense of power that goes with the office or position they hold, is the aphrodisiac of their dreams.

No wonder they smile, shake hands and insincerely kiss babies on the campaign trail, for in doing so, they are taking power, vote by vote, from the very people they desire to govern (the word "rule" comes to mind as a suitable synonym in this case, for these days there is little difference between governing and ruling).

Sheep and Taxes

BUT – despite their honeyed words and oft-repeated promises, the vast majority do not govern for the true good of their people, any more than a farmer tends his flock or his herd for the benefit of his cattle and sheep.

I speak from experience here, having worked on farms long ago, and briefly owned a farm before emigrating to the US.)

We don't need to take that metaphor too much further, except to liken the annual shearing of sheep to the annual payment of taxes. Sheep and people put in a year's work between each fleecing, and that is the extent of our value to those in the upper echelons of power.

That said, the Great Awakening is aptly named, and it is spreading further and further as one by one the "sheep" wake up, and begin to counterattack those who have been surreptitiously attacking our lives and liberties and our God-given right to Liberty and the pursuit of happiness.

At the tip of the spear is Donald J Trump, President of the United States of America. As such, he made his first appearance at the United Nations in 2017. He used the occasion to let world leaders know that there was a new sheriff in town.

He was not afraid to tell the world that as far as America is concerned, the days of the Globalists are over.
For that reason, and for the historical record, it is important to not only read, but to absorb what President Trump had to say when he addressed the United Nations in 2017.

It was an address you could liken to an iron fist in a velvet glove; more velvet than iron, but unmistakably telling world leaders that the United States is no longer a playground for the Globalists (italics added in some places for emphasis because he's letting the world know in no uncertain terms that America will no longer be taken advantage of).

2017 UN SPEECH

"**Mr. Secretary-General, Mr. President, world leaders and distinguished delegates, welcome to New York. It is a profound honor to stand here in my home city, as a representative of the American people, to address the people of the world.**

"As millions of our citizens continue to suffer the effects of the devastating hurricanes that have struck our country, I want to begin by expressing my appreciation to every leader in this room who has offered assistance and aid.

"The American people are strong and resilient, and they will emerge from these hardships more determined than ever before.

"Fortunately, the United States has done very well since Election Day last November 8. The stock market is at an all-time high, a record. Unemployment is at its lowest level in 16 years, and because of our regulatory and other reforms, we have more people working in the United States today than ever before.

"Companies are moving back, creating job growth the likes of which our country has not seen in a very long time, and it has just been announced that *we will be spending almost $700 billion on our military and defense. Our military will soon be the strongest it has ever been.*

"For more than 70 years, in times of war and peace, the leaders of nations, movements and religions have stood before this assembly. Like them, I intend to address some of the very serious threats before us today, but also the enormous potential waiting to be unleashed.

"We live in a time of extraordinary opportunity. Breakthroughs in science, technology and medicine are curing illnesses and solving problems that prior generations thought impossible to solve.
"But each day also brings news of growing dangers that threaten everything we cherish and value.

"Terrorists and extremists have gathered strength and spread to every region of the planet. *Rogue regimes represented in this body not only support terrorists, but threaten other nations and their own people with the most destructive weapons known to humanity.*
"*Authority and authoritarian powers seek to collapse the values, the systems and alliances that prevented conflict and tilted the world toward freedom since World War II.*
"*International criminal networks traffic drugs, weapons, people; force dislocation and mass migration; threaten our borders. And new forms of aggression exploit technology to menace our citizens.*

"To put it simply, we meet at a time of both immense promise and great peril.

"It is entirely up to us whether we lift the world to new heights or let it fall into a valley of disrepair. We have it in our power, should we so choose, to lift millions from poverty, to help our citizens realize their dreams and to ensure that new generations of children are raised free from violence, hatred and fear.

"This institution was founded in the aftermath of two world wars to help shape this better future. It was based on the vision that diverse nations could cooperate to protect their sovereignty, preserve their security and promote their prosperity.

"It was in the same period, exactly 70 years ago, that the United States developed the Marshall Plan to help restore Europe. Those three beautiful pillars, they're pillars of peace: sovereignty, security and prosperity.

"The Marshall Plan was built on the noble idea that the whole world is safer when nations are strong, independent and free. As President Truman said in his message to Congress at that time, "our support of European recovery is in full accord with our support of the United Nations. The success of the United Nations depends upon the independent strength of its members."

"To overcome the perils of the present and to achieve the promise of the future, we must begin with the wisdom of the past. Our success depends on a coalition of strong and independent nations that embrace their sovereignty, to promote security, prosperity and peace for themselves and for the world.

"We do not expect diverse countries to share the same cultures, traditions or "even systems of government. But *we do expect all nations to uphold these two core sovereign duties: to respect the interests of their own people and the rights of every other sovereign nation.*

"This is the beautiful vision of this institution, and this is the foundation for cooperation and success. Strong, sovereign nations let diverse countries with different values, different cultures and different dreams not just coexist, but work side by side on the basis of mutual respect. Strong, sovereign nations let their people take ownership of the future and control their own destiny, and strong, sovereign nations allow individuals to flourish in the fullness of the life intended by God.

"In America, we do not seek to impose our way of life on anyone, but rather to let it shine as an example for everyone to watch. This week gives our country a special reason to take pride in that example.

"We are celebrating the 230th anniversary of our beloved Constitution, the oldest constitution still in use in the world today. This timeless document has been the foundation of peace, prosperity and freedom for the Americans, and for countless millions around the globe whose own countries have found inspiration in its respect for human nature, human dignity and the rule of law.

"The greatest (sic) in the United States Constitution is its first three, beautiful words. They are "We the people." Generations of Americans have sacrificed to maintain the promise of those words, the promise of our country and of our great history.

"In America the people govern, the people rule and the people are sovereign.

"I was elected not to take power, but to give power to the American people where it belongs.

"In foreign affairs, we are renewing this founding principle of sovereignty. Our government's first duty is to its people, to our citizens, to serve their needs, to ensure their safety, to preserve their rights and to defend their values.

"As president of the United States, I will always put America first, just like you, as the leaders of your countries, will always and should always put your countries first.

"All responsible leaders have an obligation to serve their own citizens, and the nation-state remains the best vehicle for elevating the human condition.

"But making a better life for our people also requires us to work together in close harmony and unity to create a more safe and peaceful future for all people.

"The United States will forever be a great friend to the world, and especially to its allies. But we can no longer be taken advantage of, or enter into a one-sided deal where the United States gets nothing in return.

"As long as I hold this office, I will defend America's interests above all else. But in fulfilling our obligations to our own nations, we also realize that it's in everyone's interest to seek a future where all nations can be sovereign, prosperous and secure.

"America does more than speak for the values expressed in the United Nations charter. Our citizens have paid the ultimate price to defend our freedom and the freedom of many nations represented in this great hall. America's devotion is measured on the battlefields where our young men and women have fought and sacrificed alongside of our allies, from the beaches of Europe, to the deserts of the Middle East, to the jungles of Asia.

"It is an eternal credit to the American character that even after we and our allies emerged victorious from the bloodiest war in history, we did not seek territorial expansion or attempt to oppose and (sic) impose our way of life on others.

"Instead, we helped build institutions such as this one to defend the sovereignty, security and prosperity for all.

"For the diverse nations of the world, this is our hope. We want harmony and friendship, not conflict and strife. We are guided by outcomes, not ideology. We have a policy of principled realism rooted in shared goals, interests and values.

"That *realism forces us to confront the question facing every leader and nation in this room. It is a question we cannot escape or avoid. We will (sic) slide down the path of complacency, numb to the chal-*

lenges, threats and even wars that we face, or do we have enough strength and pride to confront those dangers today so that our citizens can enjoy peace and prosperity tomorrow?

"If we desire to lift up our citizens, if we aspire to the approval of history, then we must fulfill our sovereign duties to the people we faithfully represent.

"We must protect our nations, their interests and their futures. *We must reject threats to sovereignty,* from the Ukraine to the South China Sea. We must uphold respect for law, respect for borders and respect for culture, and the peaceful engagement these allow.

"And just as the founders of this body intended, *we must work together and confront together those who threaten us with chaos, turmoil and terror.*

"The scourge of our planet today is a small group of rogue regimes that violate every principle on which the United Nations is based. They respect neither their own citizens, nor the sovereign rights of their countries.

"If the righteous many do not confront the wicked few, then evil will triumph. When decent people and nations become bystanders to history, the forces of destruction only gather power and strength.

"No one has shown more contempt for other nations and for the well-being of their own people than the depraved regime in North Korea. It is responsible for the starvation deaths of millions of North Koreans, and for the imprisonment, torture, killing and oppression of countless more.

"We were all witness to the regime's deadly abuse when an innocent American college student, Otto Warmbier, was returned to

America only to die a few days later. We saw it in the assassination of the dictator's brother using banned nerve agents in an international airport. We know it kidnapped a sweet 13-year-old Japanese girl from a beach in her own country to enslave her as a language tutor for North Korea's spies.

"If this is not twisted enough, now *North Korea's reckless pursuit of nuclear weapons and ballistic missiles threatens the entire world with unthinkable loss of human life. It is an outrage that some nations would not only trade with such a regime, but would arm, supply and financially support a country that imperils the world with nuclear conflict.*

"No nation on Earth has an interest in seeing this band of criminals arm itself with nuclear weapons and missiles.

"The United States has great strength and patience, but if it is forced to defend itself or its allies, we will have no choice but to totally destroy North Korea. "Rocket Man" is on a suicide mission for himself and for his regime.

"The United States is ready, willing and able. But hopefully, this will not be necessary.

"That's what the United Nations is all about. That's what the United Nations is for. Let's see how they do.
"It is time for North Korea to realize that the denuclearization is its only acceptable future.

"The United Nations Security Council recently held two unanimous 15-to-nothing votes adopting hard-hitting resolutions against North Korea, and I want to thank China and Russia for joining the vote to impose sanctions, along with all of the other members of the Security Council. Thank you to all involved.

"But we must do much more. It is time for all nations to work together to isolate the Kim regime until it ceases its hostile behavior.

"We face this decision not only in North Korea. It is far past time for the nations of the world to confront another reckless regime, one that speaks openly of mass murder, vowing death to America, destruction to Israel and ruin for many leaders and nations in this room.

"The Iranian government masks a corrupt dictatorship behind the false guise of a democracy. It has turned a wealthy country with a rich history and culture into an economically depleted rogue state whose chief exports are violence, bloodshed and chaos.

"The longest suffering victims of Iran's leaders are in fact its own people. Rather than use its resources to improve Iranian lives, its oil profits go to fund Hezbollah and other terrorists that kill innocent Muslims and attack their peaceful Arab and Israeli neighbors.

"This wealth, which rightly belongs to Iran's people, also goes to shore up Bashar al-Assad's dictatorship, fuel Yemen's civil war and undermine peace throughout the entire Middle East.

"We cannot let a murderous regime continue these destabilizing activities while building dangerous missiles, and we cannot abide by an agreement if it provides cover for the eventual construction of a nuclear program.

"The Iran deal was one of the worst and most one-sided transactions the United States has ever entered into. Frankly, that deal is an embarrassment to the United States, and I don't think you've heard the last of it, believe me.

"It is time for the entire world to join us in demanding that Iran's government end its pursuit of death and destruction. It is time for the regime to free all Americans and citizens of other nations that they have unjustly detained. And above all, Iran's government must stop supporting terrorists, begin serving its own people and respect the sovereign rights of its neighbors.

"The entire world understands that the good people of Iran want change and, other than the vast military power of the United States, that Iran's people are what their leaders fear the most. This is what causes the regime to restrict internet access, tear down satellite dishes, shoot unarmed student protesters and imprison political reformists.

"Oppressive regimes cannot endure forever, and the day will come when the people will face a choice. Will they continue down the path of poverty, bloodshed and terror, or will the Iranian people return to the nation's proud roots as a center of civilization, culture and wealth, where their people can be happy and prosperous once again?

"The Iranian regime's support for terror is in stark contrast to the recent commitments of many of its neighbors to fight terrorism and halt its finance.

"In Saudi Arabia early last year, I was greatly honored to address the leaders of more than 50 Arab and Muslim nations. We agreed that all responsible nations must work together to confront terrorists and the Islamic extremism that inspires them.

"We will stop radical Islamic terrorism because we cannot allow it to tear up our nation, and indeed, to tear up the entire world. We must deny the terrorists safe haven, transit, funding and any form of support for their vile and sinister ideology. We must drive them out of our nations.

"It is time to expose and hold responsible those countries who support and finance terror groups like AL-Qaida, Hezbollah, the Taliban and others that slaughter innocent people.

"The United States and our allies are working together throughout the Middle East to crush the loser terrorists and stop the re-emergence of safe havens they use to launch attacks on all of our people.

"Last month, I announced a new strategy for victory in the fight against this evil in Afghanistan. *From now on, our security interests will dictate the length and scope of military operations, not arbitrary benchmarks and timetables set up by politicians.* I have also totally changed the rules of engagement in our fight against the Taliban and other terrorist groups.

"In Syria and Iraq, we have made big gains toward lasting defeat of ISIS. In fact, our country has achieved more against ISIS in the last eight months than it has in many, many years combined. We seek the DE-escalation of the Syrian conflict and a political solution that honors the will of the Syrian people.
"The actions of the criminal regime of Bashar AL-Assad, including the use of chemical weapons against his own citizens, even innocent children, shock the conscience of every decent person. No society can be safe if banned chemical weapons are allowed to spread. That is why the United States carried out a missile strike on the air base that launched the attack.

"We appreciate the efforts of the United Nations agencies that are providing vital humanitarian assistance in areas liberated from ISIS, and we especially thank Jordan, Turkey and Lebanon for their role in hosting refugees from the Syrian conflict.

"The United States is a compassionate nation, and has spent billions and billions of dollars in helping to support this effort. We seek an approach to refugee resettlement that is designed to help these horribly treated people, and which enables their eventual return to their home countries to be part of the rebuilding process.

"For the cost of resettling one refugee in the United States, we can assist more than 10 in their home region. Out of the goodness of our hearts, we offer financial assistance to hosting countries in the region, and we support recent agreements of the G-20 nations that will seek to host refugees as close to their home countries as possible. This is the safe, responsible and humanitarian approach.

"For decades, the United States has dealt with migration challenges. Here in the Western Hemisphere, we have learned that over the long term, uncontrolled migration is deeply unfair to both the sending and the receiving countries.

"For the sending countries, it reduces domestic pressure to pursue needed political and economic reform, and drains them of the human capital necessary to motivate and implement those reforms.

"For the receiving countries, the substantial costs of uncontrolled migration are borne overwhelmingly by low-income citizens whose concerns are often ignored by both media and government.

"I want to salute the work of the United Nations in seeking to address the problems that cause people to flee from their homes. The United Nations and African Union led peacekeeping missions to have (sic) invaluable contributions in stabilizing conflicts in Africa.

"The United States continues to lead the world in humanitarian assistance, including famine prevention and relief in South Sudan, Somalia, and northern Nigeria and Yemen. We have invested in better health and opportunity all over the world, through programs like PEPFAR, which funds AIDS relief; the President's Malaria Initiative; the Global Health Security Agenda; the Global Fund to End Modern Slavery; and the Women Entrepreneurs Finance Initiative, part of our commitment to empowering women all across the globe.

"We also thank – thank you. *We also thank the secretary general for recognizing that the United Nations must reform if it is to be an effective partner in confronting threats to sovereignty, security and prosperity.*

"Too often, the focus of this organization has not been on results, but on bureaucracy and process. In some cases, states that seek to subvert this institution's noble ends have hijacked the very systems that are supposed to advance them.

"For example, it is a massive source of embarrassment to the United Nations that some governments with egregious human rights records sit on the UN. Human Rights Council.

"The United States is one out of 193 countries in the United Nations, and yet we pay 22 percent of the entire budget and more. In fact, we pay far more than anybody realizes.

"The United States bears an unfair cost burden. But, to be fair, if it could actually accomplish all of its stated goals, especially the goal of peace, this investment would easily be well worth it.

"Major portions of the world are in conflict, and some, in fact, are going to hell. But the powerful people in this room, under the guidance and auspices of the United Nations, can solve many of these vicious and complex problems.

"The American people hope that one day soon the United Nations can be a much more accountable and effective advocate for human dignity and freedom around the world.

"In the meantime, we believe that no nation should have to bear a disproportionate share of the burden militarily or financially. Nations of the world must take a greater role in promoting secure and prosperous societies in their own regions.

"That is why in the Western Hemisphere, the United States has stood against the corrupt, destabilizing regime in Cuba and embraced the enduring dream of the Cuban people to live in freedom.

"My administration recently announced that we will not lift sanctions on the Cuban government until it makes fundamental reforms.

"We have also imposed tough, calibrated sanctions on the socialist Maduro regime in Venezuela, which has brought a once-thriving nation to the brink of total collapse.

"The socialist dictatorship of Nicolas Maduro has inflicted terrible pain and suffering on the good people of that country. This corrupt regime destroyed a prosperous nation by imposing a failed ideology that has produced poverty and misery everywhere it has been tried. To make matters worse, Maduro has defied his own people, stealing power from their elected representatives to preserve his disastrous rule.

"The Venezuelan people are starving and their country is collapsing. Their democratic institutions are being destroyed. This situation is completely unacceptable, and we cannot stand by and watch. As a responsible neighbor and friend, we and all others have a goal. That goal is to help them regain their freedom, recover their country and restore their democracy.

"I would like to thank leaders in this room for condemning the regime and providing vital support to the Venezuelan people.

"The United States has taken important steps to hold the

regime accountable. We are prepared to take further action if the government of Venezuela persists on its path to impose authoritarian rule on the Venezuelan people.

"We are fortunate to have incredibly strong and healthy trade relationships with many of the Latin American countries gathered here today. Our economic bond forms a critical foundation for advancing peace and prosperity for all of our people and all of our neighbors.

"I ask every country represented here today to be prepared to do more to address this very real crisis. We call for the full restoration of democracy and political freedoms in Venezuela.
"The problem in Venezuela is not that socialism has been poorly implemented, but that socialism has been faithfully implemented.

"From the Soviet Union to Cuba to Venezuela, wherever true socialism or communism has been adopted, it has delivered anguish and devastation and failure. Those who preach the tenets of these discredited ideologies only contribute to the continued suffering of the people who live under these cruel systems.

"America stands with every person living under a brutal regime. *Our respect for sovereignty is also a call for action. All people deserve a government that cares for their safety, their interests and their well-being, including their prosperity.*

"In America, we seek stronger ties of business and trade with all nations of goodwill. But this trade must be fair and it must be reciprocal. *For too long, the American people were told that mammoth multinational trade deals, unaccountable international tribunals and powerful global bureaucracies were the best way to promote their success.*

"But as those promises flowed, millions of jobs vanished and thousands of factories disappeared. Others gamed the system and broke the rules, and our great middle class, once the bedrock of American prosperity, was forgotten and left behind. But they are forgotten no more and they will never be forgotten again.
"While America will pursue cooperation and commerce with other nations, we are renewing our commitment to the first duty of every government, the duty of (sic) our citizens. This bond is the source of America's strength and that of every responsible nation represented here today.

"If this organization is to have any hope of successfully confronting the challenges before us, it will depend, as President Truman said some 70 years ago, on the independent strength of its members.

"If we are to embrace the opportunities of the future and overcome the present dangers together, there can be no substitute for strong, sovereign and independent nations; nations that are rooted in their histories and invested in their destinies; nations that seek allies to befriend not enemies to conquer, and most important of all, nations that are home to patriots, to men and women who are willing to sacrifice for their countries, their fellow citizens and for all that is best in the human spirit.

"In remembering the great victory that led to this body's founding, we must never forget that those heroes who fought against evil also fought for the nations that they loved. Patriotism led the Poles to die to save Poland, the French to fight for a free France and the Brits to stand strong for Britain.

"Today, if we do not invest ourselves, our hearts and our minds in our nations – if we will not build strong families, safe communities and healthy societies for ourselves – no one can do it for us. We cannot wait for someone else, for faraway countries or far-off bureaucracies. We can't do it.

"We must solve our problems to build our prosperity, to secure our future, or we will build (sic) vulnerable to decay, domination and defeat.

"The true question for the United Nations today, for people all over the world who hope for better lives for themselves and their children, is a basic one: Are we still patriots? Do we love our nations enough to protect their sovereignty and to take ownership of their futures? Do we revere them enough to defend their interests, preserve their cultures and ensure a peaceful world for their citizens?

"One of the greatest American patriots, John Adams, wrote that the American Revolution was effected before the war commenced. The revolution was in the minds and hearts of the people. That was the moment when America awoke, when we looked around and understood that we were a nation. We realized who we were, what we valued and what we would give our lives to defend. From its very first moments, the American story is the story of what is possible when people take ownership of their future.

"The United States of America has been among the greatest forces for good in the history of the world and the greatest defenders of sovereignty, security and prosperity for all. Now we are calling for a great reawakening of nations, for the revival of their spirits, their pride, their people and their patriotism.

"History is asking us whether we are up to the task. Our answer will be a renewal of will, a rediscovery of resolve and a rebirth of devotion. *We need to defeat* **the enemies of humanity** *and unlock the potential of life itself.* Our hope is a word and (sic) world of proud, independent nations that embrace their duties, seek friendship, respect others and make common cause in the greatest shared interest of all, a future of dignity and peace for the people of this wonderful Earth.

"This is the true vision of the United Nations, the ancient wish of every people and the deepest yearning that lives inside every sacred soul.

"So let this be our mission and let this be our message to the world: We will fight together, sacrifice together and stand together for peace, for freedom, for justice, for family, for humanity and for the almighty God who made us all.

"Thank you. God bless you. God bless the nations of the world, and God bless the United States of America. Thank you very much."

B.O. – UNFORGIVEN

Speaking of Globalists and their desire to take over America, President Trump has openly said he will never forgive Obama for the way he let the military run down.

Evidence of his depth of feeling can be seen in his refusal to unveil the portrait of Obama in the White House.

Not only did Obama dismiss many high-ranking patriotic officers who disagreed with his policies, he also turned a blind eye to the fact that steel imported from China for ship-building and tanks, was deliberately manufactured by China at 40% below specified strength.

At a televised (by Fox) Town Hall meeting in early March 2020, President Trump also said when he came into office he was told by the military that going to war, which was a possibility because of threats by North Korea, would be a very bad move. Why? Because, said his military top brass, "we don't have any ammunition." That's how much Obama had weakened the US military.

Asked at the Town Hall whether he had spoken with Obama, he responded by saying they had met once during the transition, and then, said the president "at the funeral of President (GHW) Bush we sat beside Obama. I said 'Hello' and when it was over I said 'goodbye.'"

There are a number of things that President Trump has said he will never forgive Obama for.

The way in which the military was run down is just one of them, and this president has not revealed all of the others that might be on his mind. However, what he did do on attaining office was to immediately start rebuilding the military, eventually budgeting something like several trillion dollars to rapidly make America's forces "the most powerful in the world."

His decision to create the new Space Force is another example of his determination to ensure that America has the edge when it comes to *all theaters* of war.

His reference in his 2017 address to the UN about *"new forms of aggression* (that) *exploit technology to menace our citizens"* may perhaps have hinted at the advances other countries, and secret Deep State projects have made in placing high-tech weaponry in space.

Perhaps too it included the push by telecommunications giants to introduce 5G technology around the globe – or to research into bio-weapons such as viruses.
The president has insisted on beefing up the military, while at the same time hoping to avoid war, which in part can be seen in his creation of personal relationships with both Kim Jong Un of North Korea ("we would have immediately been at war with North Korea if the other side had won," he said) and China's Xi.

He has also said nobody is tougher on Russia than him.

While it might be hard to believe that Trump, Xi and Putin are working together to get rid of the cabals that have infected their countries, there have been some hints to that effect.

PUTIN – ANTI NWO?

As for Russia, what we never hear from America's propaganda media is that over the past few years President Putin has progressively moved against the Rothschild-controlled banking system in his country.

This requires some serious research because I must admit this information was as much a surprise to me as to anybody.

So to confirm by seeking more than one source, a search for "Putin+Rothschild+bank" yields numerous reports going back as far as 2013. It appears that Putin is definitely battling the New World Order.

The first return from that search brings up an article by newspunch.com (https://bit.ly/3cd4H3l) dated June 1 2016. It starts by saying "Putin recently reminded his cabinet that he paid off the Rothschild's debt and 'grabbed them by the scruff of the neck and kicked them out Russia's back door.'

This meeting featured the President pounding his fist on the table and vowing to destroy the New World Order, and according to a Kremlin source Putin is making great strides towards this goal."

Frankly, that sounds a bit made up, as such quotes which are not sourced can just as easily be the reporter's imagination running wild. Even so, there may well be some accuracy within the story itself, but it always pays to look for more than one source, keeping in mind that reporters do tend to bounce off each others' articles and say similar things, without always getting down to revealing where the original information came from.

Do that search yourself and you'll likely find about 20 results on the first page. Scroll down past gmmuk.com, www.dzig.de, geopolitics.co, csglobe.com and a few others, and you get to bloomberg.com and an opinion article from June 7 2018 (https://bloom.bg/2L4YXgc).

In what you can read before being told you must be a paying subscriber to read the rest, there is no mention of Putin getting rid of the Rothschilds. But the headline just might be a real clue.

It says "Putin's Creeping Nationalization of Banks – The slow-motion grab of the sector by the state continues, though the central bank won't admit it."

Well, we know that Mike Bloomberg is a total Globalist who can afford to "buy" as many as 40 politicians into government via massive donations (as he stated in one of the recent debates), and spend close to a billion dollars (according to a President Trump tweet) on a failed presidential bid himself.

He's a Democrat and a Globalist, so it should be no surprise that Bloomberg writers don't go anywhere near the subject of Putin himself removing his country from Rothschild control of Russia's economy via its control of much of the banking system.

On the other hand, if we go back to the NewsPunch site, and click the "about" link, we find NewsPunch has been active since 2014 "covering the headlines mainstream outlets shy away from." It gets up to five million views a month.

Checking the "about" link on any website we're unfamiliar with is, in my experience, step one in figuring out whether the site is genuine, or possibly a psyop, a deliberately satirical one, or perhaps just some individual offering personal opinions unsubstantiated by any associated sources.

While it is nice to find many sites that are doing their best to cover subjects the propaganda media ignores, the Deep State/Globalists nevertheless do use the Internet to try and counter such negative coverage.

Now, having spent a half hour perusing the NewsPunch site, seeing articles contributed by writers all over the world, and reading their statement that "While our job is to bring audiences the truth, we will occasionally make mistakes ... When we do, we commit to correcting our errors in a timely manner ..." it has passed the sniff test. Therefore, in pursuit of verification that Putin has indeed ousted the Rothschilds, we can use the NewsPunch search box with just one word – Putin.

This brings up 179 pages of Putin articles – amounting to something over 1000 stories in the past six years. Refine the search to Putin+Rothschild and you reduce the return to five pages of really enlightening articles about how Putin has spent years removing the Rothschild influence from Russia.

One of their articles (Sept 7 2016), supported by a picture of a wrecked vehicle, says the New World Order (Rothschilds) attempted to assassinate Putin by setting up a head-on collision involving a Mercedes and Putin's official vehicle – except that Putin changed cars at the last minute (https://bit.ly/2zgUUuI).

Unfortunately his most-trusted driver in the target vehicle was killed in the collision. Strangely, there is no mention of the occupant or driver of the other vehicle. Was there an occupant, or was the car remotely controlled?

The possibility is based on past reports of American journalist

Michael Hastings dying in a car wreck when his car sped up to over 100 mph before hitting a roadside tree. Conjecture – the vehicle was taken over by remote control.

Hastings just happened to be about to publish a revealing article in Rolling Stone about the NSA. Again, a duckduckgo search for "journalist dies in car crash" brings up results linking to that incident. And more.

Surprisingly, the search engine also returns references to Jessica Savitch of NBC-TV killed in a car accident (1983); Bob Simon of '60 minutes killed in car crash (2015); Serena Shim, war correspondent, killed in car crash (1985); Daphne Galizia (lead reporter re Panama Papers) killed by car bomb in Malta (2017); Pulitzer Prize-winning journalist David Halberstam killed in car crash (2007); India journalists die in car crash (Feb 2020).

While it may be argued that aside from the Malta car bomb assassination the rest were genuine accidents, assassinations are indisputably part and parcel of the Deep State playbook.

Threats against family members are another. A third would be compromising videos and blackmail, using such frontmen as Hugh Herffner and his Playboy empire, or the depraved Jeffrey Epstein and his "orgy island" which was visited countless times by the likes of Bill Clinton, with Britain's Prince Andrew also involved in Epstein's circle of abusers of women and children.

Within all of the above, I for one can see the shadow hand of the Deep State and their protocols.

SOTU 2018

I was in two minds about including President Trump's 2018 State of the Union (SOTU) address.

Initially I wrote "Rather than trying to take in his full speech, some relevant excerpts show us what America had gone through and what he had achieved in his first twelve months in office."

But as I was deleting paragraph after paragraph, eliminating anecdote after anecdote about the real people and real heroes he honored on that occasion, I realized I was no longer a mainstream reporter trying to condense a speech into a few highlights in print or a 60-second clip on television.

Those days are long gone, and good riddance. Such truncated "news" has created a world of people who get their information in controlled sound bites and statements of opinion that are far removed from what the full story is really about.

This book is intended to be not just an edifying tome about the Illuminati and the Deep State, but also a book of record – an archive for future generations to ponder, to discuss, and to hope that this time in history will never be repeated.

Therefore, the full SOTU address of 2018 follows shortly.

Q has rightly said in one or more of his posts that "this is a crossroads in the history of civilization." So true. The road "they" were taking us down could truly have been the end of civilization as we have known it, replaced by every sort of overt and covert tyranny and control you can imagine.

The elite would have been able to carry on their secretive human sacrifice and their Satanic rituals while we would continue to be nothing more than their useful serfs. Globalists would have controlled the world economy, the world food supply, our health as well, and every aspect of government, and to be sure, they might well have reduced the population to the 500,000,000 mentioned on the Georgia Guidestones.

As they say among Qanons, taking the red pill, or being redpilled, begins the great personal awakening, but the truth can indeed be hard to swallow.

A far more palatable truth is that certain patriots, including those in military intelligence where they no doubt had access to systems that vacuum up all sorts of data off the Internet, developed a plan – or two.

Perhaps, knowing what the Cabal and its bought politicians were up to, they discussed the possibility of a military coup, which has been an age-old way of deposing those in power. Perhaps they considered a coup against Obama, or potentially Hillary.

Having never played war games myself, I can nevertheless imagine these people realizing that they must develop a strategy – a "war game" if you will – that would achieve their goal without such a coup, but which would nevertheless be a silent and sometimes deadly war using a variety of tactics to progressively encircle and take down the enemy.

That encircling can be seen as the real awakening, one by one, of people like you and me, people around the world, not just in

America, who have red pilled themselves and have now become a real force to reckon with.

No guns are involved. No violence is suggested. Their ammunition is knowledge, and the more it spreads, the more the Globalists have to fear.

They know so well that their greatest enemy is an awakened public – and then, to the great astonishment and chagrin of the Evil Ones, Hillary Clinton lost the 2016 election.
President Trump was inaugurated.
By 2018 he had much to report.

SOTU SPEECH

"**M**r. Speaker, Mr. Vice President, Members of Congress, first lady of the United States, and my fellow Americans, less than one year has passed since I first stood at this podium in this majestic chamber to speak on behalf of the American people and to address their concerns, their hopes and their dreams.

"That night, our new Administration had already taken very swift action. A new tide of optimism was already sweeping across our land. Each day since, we have gone forward with a clear vision and a righteous mission: to make America great again for all Americans.

"Over the last year, we have made incredible progress and achieved extraordinary success. We have faced challenges we expected and others we could never have imagined. We have shared in the heights of victory and the pains of hardship. We have endured floods and fires and storms. But through it all, we have seen the beauty of America's soul and the steel in America's spine.

"Each test has forged new American heroes to remind us who we are and show us what we can be. We saw the volunteers of the Cajun Navy, racing to the rescue with their fishing boats to save people in the aftermath of a totally devastating hurricane. We saw strangers shielding strangers from a hail of gunfire on the Las Vegas strip. We heard tales of Americans, like Coast Guard Petty Officer Ashlee Leppert, who is here tonight in the gallery with Melania.

"Ashlee was aboard one of the first helicopters on the scene in Houston during the Hurricane Harvey. Through 18 hours of wind and rain, Ashlee braved live power lines and deep water to help save more than 40 lives. Ashlee, we all thank you. Thank you very much.

"We heard about Americans like firefighter David Dahlberg. He's here with us, also. David faced down walls of flame to rescue almost 60 children trapped at a California summer camp threatened by those devastating wildfires.

"To everyone still recovering in Texas, Florida, Louisiana, Puerto Rico, and the Virgin Islands, everywhere, we are with you, we love you, and we always will pull through together always. Thank you to David and the brave people of California. Thank you very much, David. Great job.

"Some trials over the past year touched this chamber very personally. With us tonight is one of the toughest people ever to serve in this House, a guy who took a bullet, almost died, and was back to work three-and-a-half months later, the legend from Louisiana, Congressman Steve Scalise. And together we are building a safe, strong, and proud America.

"Since the election, we have created 2.4 million new jobs, including... including 200,000 new jobs in manufacturing alone. Tremendous number. After years and years of wage stagnation, we are finally seeing rising wages.

"Unemployment claims have hit a 45-year low. And something I'm very proud of, African-American unemployment stands at the lowest rate ever recorded. And Hispanic-American unemployment has also reached the lowest levels in history.

"Small-business confidence is at an all-time high. The stock market has smashed one record after another, gaining $8 trillion and more in value in just this short period of time. The great news... the great news for Americans, 401K, retirement, pension, and college savings accounts have gone through the roof.

"And just as I promised the American people from this podium 11 months ago, we enacted the biggest tax cuts and reforms in American history. Our massive tax cuts provide tremendous relief for the middle class and small business.

"To lower tax rates for hardworking Americans, we nearly doubled the standard deduction for everyone. Now the first $24,000 earned by a married couple is completely tax-free. We also doubled the child tax credit. A typical family of four making $75,000 will see their tax bill reduced by $2,000, slashing their tax bill in half. In April, this will be the last time you will ever file under the old and very broken system, and millions of Americans will have more take-home pay starting next month. A lot more.

"We eliminated an especially cruel tax that fell mostly on Americans making less than $50,000 a year, forcing them to pay tremendous penalties simply because they couldn't afford government-ordered health plans.

"We repealed the core of the disastrous Obamacare. The individual mandate is now gone. We slashed the business tax rate from 35 percent all the way down to 21 percent, so American companies can compete and win against anyone else anywhere in the world. These changes alone are estimated to increase average family income by more than $4,000. A lot of money.

"Small businesses have also received a massive tax cut and can now deduct 20 percent of their business income. Here tonight are Steve Staub and Sandy Keplinger of Staub Manufacturing, a small beautiful business in Ohio. They've just finished the best year in their 20-year history. Because of tax reform, they are handing out raises, hiring an additional 14 people, and expanding into the building next door. Good feeling.

"One of Staub's employees, Corey Adams, is also with us tonight. Corey is an all-American worker. He supported himself through high school, lost his job during the 2008 recession, and was later hired by Staub, where he trained to become a welder. Like many hardworking Americans, Corey plans to invest his tax cut raise into his new home and his two daughters' education. Corey, please stand. And he's a great welder. I was told that by the man that owns that company that's doing so well, so congratulations, Corey.

"Since we passed tax cuts, roughly 3 million workers have already gotten tax cut bonuses, many of them thousands and thousands of dollars per worker. And it's getting more every month, every week.

"Apple has just announced it plans to invest a total of $350 billion in America and hire another 20,000 workers. And just a little while ago, Exxon Mobil announced a $50 billion investment in the United States. Just a little while ago.

"This, in fact, is our new American moment. There has never been a better time to start living the American dream.

"So to every citizen watching at home tonight, no matter where you've been or where you've come from, this is your time. If you work hard, if you believe in yourself, if you believe in America, then you can dream anything, you can be anything, and together, we can achieve absolutely anything.

"Tonight, I want to talk about what kind of future we are going to have and what kind of a nation we are going to be.

"All of us, together, as one team, one people, and one American family can do anything. We all share the same home, the same heart, the same destiny, and the same great American flag.

"Together, we are rediscovering the American way. In America, we know that faith and family, not government and bureaucracy, are the center of American life. The motto is "in God we trust." And we celebrate our police, our military, and our amazing veterans as heroes who deserve our total and unwavering support.

"Here tonight is Preston Sharp, a 12-year-old boy from Redding, California, who noticed that veterans' graves were not marked with flags on Veterans Day. He decided all by himself to change that and started a movement that has now placed 40,000 flags at the graves of our great heroes. Preston, a job well done.

"Young patriots like Preston teach all of us about our civic duty as Americans. And I met Preston a little while ago, and he is something very special, that I can tell you. Great future. Thank you very much for all you've done, Preston. Thank you very much.

"Preston's reverence for those who have served our nation reminds us why we salute our flag, why we put our hands on our hearts for the Pledge of Allegiance, and why we proudly stand for the national anthem.

"Americans love their country. And they deserve a government that shows them the same love and loyalty in return. For the last year, we have sought to restore the bonds of trust between our citizens and their government. Working with the Senate, we are appointing judges who will interpret the Constitution as written, including a great new Supreme Court justice and more circuit court judges than any new administration in the history of our country.

"We are totally defending our Second Amendment and have taken historic actions to protect religious liberty. And we are serving our brave veterans, including giving our veterans choice in their health care decisions.

"Last year, Congress also passed, and I signed, the landmark VA Accountability Act. Since its passage, my administration has already removed more than 1,500 VA employees who failed to give our veterans the care they deserve, and we are hiring talented people who love our vets as much as we do.

"And I will not stop until our veterans are properly taken care of, which has been my promise to them from the very beginning of this great journey. All Americans deserve accountability and respect, and that's what we are giving to our wonderful heroes, our veterans. Thank you.
"So tonight, I call on Congress to empower every cabinet secretary with the authority to reward good workers and to remove federal employees who undermine the public trust or fail the American people.

"In our drive to make Washington accountable, we have eliminated more regulations in our first year than any administration in the history of our country. We have ended the war on American energy, and we have ended the war on beautiful clean coal. We are now very proudly an exporter of energy to the world.

"In Detroit, I halted government mandates that crippled America's great, beautiful autoworkers so that we can get Motor City revving its engines again. And that's what's happening. Many car companies are now building and expanding plants in the United States, something we haven't seen for decades.

"Chrysler is moving a major plant from Mexico to Michigan. Toyota and Mazda are opening up a plant in Alabama, a big one. And we haven't seen this in a long time. It's all coming back. Very soon, auto plants and other plants will be opening up all over our country.

"This is all news Americans are totally unaccustomed to hearing. For many years, companies and jobs were only leaving us. But now they are roaring back, they're coming back. They want to be where the action is. They want to be in the United States of America. That's where they want to be.

"Exciting progress is happening every single day. To speed access to breakthrough cures and affordable generic drugs, last year the FDA approved more new and generic drugs and medical devices than ever before in our country's history. We also believe that patients with terminal conditions and terminal illness should have access to experimental treatment immediately that could potentially save their lives.

"People who are terminally ill should not have to go from country to country to seek a cure. I want to give them a chance right here at home. It's time for Congress to give these wonderful, incredible Americans the right to try.

"One of my greatest priorities is to reduce the price of prescription drugs. In many other countries, these drugs cost far less than what we pay in the United States. And it's very, very unfair. That is why I have directed my administration to make fixing the injustice of high drug prices one of my top priorities for the year. And prices will come down substantially. Watch.

"America has also finally turned the page on decades of unfair trade deals that sacrificed our prosperity and shipped away our companies, our jobs, and our wealth. Our nation has lost its wealth, but we're getting it back so fast. The era of economic surrender is totally over. From now on, we expect trading relationships to be fair and, very importantly, reciprocal.

"We will work to fix bad trade deals and negotiate new ones. And they'll be good ones, but they'll be fair. And we will protect American workers and American intellectual property through strong enforcement of our trade rules. As we rebuild our industries, it is also time to rebuild our crumbling infrastructure.

"America is a nation of builders. We built the Empire State Building in just one year. Isn't it a disgrace that it can now take 10 years just to get a minor permit approved for the building of a simple road? I am asking both parties to come together to give us safe, fast, reliable, and modern infrastructure that our economy needs and our people deserve.

"Tonight I'm calling on Congress to produce a bill that generates at least $1.5 trillion for the new infrastructure investment that our country so desperately needs. Every federal dollar should be leveraged by partnering with state and local governments and, where appropriate, tapping into private sector investment to permanently fix the infrastructure deficit. And we can do it.

"Any bill must also streamline the permitting and approval process, getting it down to no more than two years, and perhaps even one. Together, we can reclaim our great building heritage. We will build gleaming new roads, bridges, highways, railways, and waterways all across our land. And we will do it with American heart, American hands, and American grit.

"We want every American to know the dignity of a hard day's work. We want every child to be safe in their home at night. And we want every citizen to be proud of this land that we all love so much. We can lift our citizens from welfare to work, from dependence to independence, and from poverty to prosperity.

"As… as tax cuts create new jobs, let's invest in workforce development and let's invest in job training, which we need so badly. Let's open great vocational schools so our future workers can learn a craft and realize their full potential. And let's support working families by supporting paid family leave.

"As America regains its strength, opportunity must be extended to all citizens. That is why this year we will embark on reforming our prisons to help former inmates who have served their time get a second chance at life.

"Struggling communities, especially immigrant communities, will also be helped by immigration policies that focus on the best interests of American workers and American families.

"For decades, open borders have allowed drugs and gangs to pour into our most vulnerable communities. They've allowed millions of low-wage workers to compete for jobs and wages against the poorest Americans. Most tragically, they have caused the loss of many innocent lives.
"Here tonight are two fathers and two mothers: Evelyn Rodriguez, Freddy Cuevas, Elizabeth Alvarado, and Robert Mickens. Their two teenage daughters – Kayla Cuevas and Nisa Mickens - were close friends on Long Island. But in September 2016, on the eve of Nisa's 16th birthday, such a happy time it should have been, neither of them came home.

"These two precious girls were brutally murdered while walking together in their hometown. Six members of the savage MS-13 gang have been charged with Kayla and Nisa's murders. Many of these gang members took advantage of glaring loopholes in our laws to enter the country as illegal unaccompanied alien minors and wound up in Kayla and Nisa's high school.

"Evelyn, Elizabeth, Freddy, and Robert, tonight, everyone in this chamber is praying for you. Everyone in America is grieving for you. Please stand. Thank you very much. I want you to know that 320 million hearts are right now breaking for you. We love you. Thank you. While we cannot imagine the depths of that kind of sorrow, we can make sure that other families never have to endure this kind of pain.

"Tonight, I am calling on Congress to finally close the deadly loopholes that have allowed MS-13, and other criminal gangs, to break into our country. We have proposed new legislation that will fix our immigration laws, and support our ICE and Border Patrol agents – these are great people, these are great, great people that work so hard in the midst of such danger – so that this can never happen again.

"The United States is a compassionate nation. We are proud that we do more than any other country anywhere in the world to help the needy, the struggling, and the underprivileged all over the world. But as president of the United States, my highest loyalty, my greatest compassion, my constant concern is for America's children, America's struggling workers, and America's forgotten communities. I want our youth to grow up to achieve great things. I want our poor to have their chance to rise.

"So tonight, I am extending an open hand to work with members of both parties – Democrats and Republicans – to protect our citizens of every background, color, religion, and creed.

"My duty, and the sacred duty of every elected official in this chamber, is to defend Americans, to protect their safety, their families, their communities, and their right to the American dream. Because Americans are dreamers, too.

"Here tonight is one leader in the effort to defend our country, Homeland Security Investigations Special Agent Celestino Martinez. He goes by DJ. And CJ. He said call me either one. So we'll call you CJ. Served 15 years in the Air Force before becoming an ICE agent and spending the last 15 years fighting gang violence and getting dangerous criminals off of our streets. Tough job.

"At one point, MS-13 leaders ordered CJ's murder, and they wanted it to happen quickly. But he did not cave to threats or to fear. Last May, he commanded an operation to track down gang members on Long Island. His team has arrested nearly 400, including more than 220 MS-13 gang members.

"And I have to tell you what the Border Patrol and ICE have done. We have sent thousands and thousands and thousands of MS-13 horrible people out of this country or into our prisons. So I just want to congratulate you, CJ. You're a brave guy. Thank you very much.

"And I asked CJ, what's the secret? He said, "We're just tougher than they are." And I like that answer. Now let's get Congress to send you – and all of the people in this great chamber have to do it, we have no choice - CJ, we're going to send you reinforcements and we're going to send them to you quickly. It's what you need.

"Over the next few weeks, the House and Senate will be voting on an immigration reform package. In recent months, my administration has met extensively with both Democrats and Republicans to craft a bipartisan approach to immigration reform. Based on these discussions, we presented Congress with a detailed proposal that should be supported by both parties as a fair compromise, one where nobody gets everything they want, but where our country gets the critical reforms it needs and must have.

"Here are the four pillars of our plan. The first pillar of our framework generously offers a path to citizenship for 1.8 million illegal immigrants who were brought here by their parents at a young age. That covers almost three times more people than the previous administration covered. Under our plan, those who meet education and work requirements, and show good moral character, will be able to become full citizens of the United States over a 12-year period.

"The second pillar fully secures the border. That means building a great wall on the southern border, and it means hiring more heroes like CJ to keep our communities safe. Crucially, our plan closes the terrible loopholes exploited by criminals and terrorists to enter our country, and it finally ends the horrible and dangerous practice of catch and release.

"The third pillar ends the visa lottery, a program that randomly hands out green cards without any regard for skill, merit, or the safety of American people. It's time to begin moving toward a merit-based immigration system, one that admits people who are skilled, who want to work, who will contribute to our society, and who will love and respect our country.

"The fourth and final pillar protects the nuclear family by ending chain migration. Under the current broken system, a single immigrant can bring in virtually unlimited numbers of distant relatives. Under our plan, we focus on the immediate family by limiting sponsorships to spouses and minor children.
This vital reform is necessary, not just for our economy, but for our security and for the future of America.

"In recent weeks, two terrorist attacks in New York were made possible by the visa lottery and chain migration. In the age of terrorism, these programs present risks we can just no longer afford. It's time to reform... these outdated immigration rules and finally bring our immigration system into the 21st century.

"These four pillars represent a down-the-middle compromise and one that will create a safe, modern, and lawful immigration system. For over 30 years, Washington has tried and failed to solve this problem. This Congress can be the one that finally makes it happen. Most importantly, these four pillars will produce legislation that fulfills my ironclad pledge to sign a bill that puts America first. So let's come together, set politics aside, and finally get the job done.

"These reforms will also support our response to the terrible crisis of opioid and drug addiction. Never before has it been like it is now. It is terrible. We have to do something about it. In 2016, we lost 64,000 Americans to drug overdoses, 174 deaths per day, seven per hour. We must get much tougher on drug dealers and pushers if we are going to succeed in stopping this scourge.

"My administration is committed to fighting the drug epidemic and helping get treatment for those in need, for those who have been so terribly hurt. The struggle will be long and it will be difficult, but as Americans always do, in the end, we will succeed, we will prevail.
"As we have seen tonight, the most difficult challenges bring out the best in America. We see a vivid expression of this truth in the story of the Holets family of New Mexico.

"Ryan Holets is 27 years old, an officer with the Albuquerque Police Department. He's here tonight with his wife, Rebecca. Thank you, Ryan. Last year, Ryan was on duty when he saw a pregnant, homeless woman preparing to inject heroin. When Ryan told her she was going to harm her unborn child, she began to weep. She told him she didn't know where to turn, but badly wanted a safe home for her baby.

"In that moment, Ryan said he felt God speak to him: 'You will do it because you can.' He heard those words. He took out a picture of his wife and their four kids. Then he went home to tell his wife, Rebecca. In an instant, she agreed to adopt. The Holets named their new daughter Hope. Ryan and Rebecca, you embody the goodness of our nation. Thank you. Thank you, Ryan and Rebecca.

"As we rebuild America's strength and confidence at home, we are also restoring our strength and standing abroad. Around the world, we face rogue regimes, terrorist groups, and rivals like China and Russia that challenge our interests, our economy, and our values. In confronting these horrible dangers, we know that weakness is the surest path to conflict, and unmatched power is the surest means to our true and great defense.

"For this reason, I am asking Congress to end the dangerous defense sequester and fully fund our great military. As part of our defense, we must modernize and rebuild our nuclear arsenal, hopefully never having to use it, but making it so strong and so powerful that it will deter any acts of aggression by any other nation or anyone else. Perhaps some day in the future there will be a magical moment when the countries of the world will get together to eliminate their nuclear weapons. Unfortunately, we are not there yet, sadly.

"Last year, I also pledged that we would work with our allies to extinguish ISIS from the face of the Earth. One year later, I am proud to report that the coalition to defeat ISIS has liberated very close to 100 percent of the territory just recently held by these killers in Iraq and in Syria and in other locations, as well. But there is much more work to be done. We will continue our fight until ISIS is defeated.

"Army Staff Sergeant Justin Peck is here tonight. Near Raqqa last November, Justin and his comrade, Chief Petty Officer Kenton Stacy, were on a mission to clear buildings that ISIS had rigged with explosive so that civilians could return to that city, hopefully soon and hopefully safely.

"Clearing the second floor of a vital hospital, Kenton Stacy was severely wounded by an explosion. Immediately, Justin bounded into the booby-trapped and unbelievably dangerous and unsafe building and found Kenton, but in very, very bad shape. He applied pressure to the wound and inserted a tube to reopen an airway. He then performed CPR for 20 straight minutes during the ground transport and maintained artificial respiration through two-and-a-half hours and through emergency surgery.

"Kenton Stacy would have died if it were not for Justin's selfless love for his fellow warrior. Tonight, Kenton is recovering in Texas. Raqqa is liberated. And Justin is wearing his new Bronze Star, with a V for Valor. Staff Sergeant Peck: All of America salutes you.

"Terrorists who do things like place bombs in civilian hospitals are evil. When possible, we have no choice but to annihilate them. When necessary, we must be able to detain and question them. But we must be clear: Terrorists are not merely criminals. They are unlawful enemy combatants. And when captured overseas, they should be treated like the terrorists they are. In the past, we have foolishly released hundreds of dangerous terrorists, only to meet them again on the battlefield, including the ISIS leader, al-Baghdadi, who we captured, who we had, who we released.

"So today, I am keeping another promise. I just signed prior to walking in an order directing Secretary Mattis - who is doing a great job, thank you... to re-examine our military detention policy and to keep open the detention facilities in Guantanamo Bay. I am asking Congress to ensure that in the fight against ISIS and Al Qaida we continue to have all necessary power to detain terrorists, wherever we chase them down, wherever we find them. And in many cases, for them it will now be Guantanamo Bay.

"At the same time, as of a few months ago, our warriors in Afghanistan have new rules of engagement. Along with their heroic Afghan partners, our military is no longer undermined by artificial timelines, and we no longer tell our enemies our plans.

"Last month, I also took an action endorsed unanimously by the U.S. Senate just months before. I recognized Jerusalem as the capital of Israel. Shortly afterwards, dozens of countries voted in the United Nations General Assembly against America's sovereign right to make this decision.

"In 2016, American taxpayers generously sent those same countries more than $20 billion in aid. That is why tonight I am asking Congress to pass legislation to help ensure American foreign assistance dollars always serve American interests and only go to friends of America, not enemies of America.

"As we strengthen friendships all around the world, we are also restoring clarity about our adversaries. When the people of Iran rose up against the crimes of their corrupt dictatorship, I did not stay silent. America stands with the people of Iran in their courageous struggle for freedom. I am asking Congress to address the fundamental flaws in the terrible Iran nuclear deal. My administration has also imposed tough sanctions on the communist and socialist dictatorships in Cuba and Venezuela.

"But no regime has oppressed its own citizens more totally or brutally than the cruel dictatorship in North Korea. North Korea's reckless pursuit of nuclear missiles could very soon threaten our homeland. We are waging a campaign of maximum pressure to prevent that from ever happening.

"Past experience has taught us that complacency and concessions only invite aggression and provocation. I will not repeat the mistakes of past administrations that got us into this very dangerous position.

"We need only look at the depraved character of the North Korean regime to understand the nature of the nuclear threat it could pose to America and to our allies.

"Otto Warmbier was a hardworking student at the University of Virginia. And a great student, he was. On his way to study abroad in Asia, Otto joined a tour to North Korea. At its conclusion, this wonderful young man was arrested and charged with crimes against the state.

"After a shameful trial, the dictatorship sentenced Otto to 15 years of hard labor, before returning him to America last June, horribly injured and on the verge of death. He passed away just days after his return.

"Otto's wonderful parents, Fred and Cindy Warmbier, are here with us tonight, along with Otto's brother and sister, Austin and Greta. Please. Incredible people. You are powerful witnesses to a menace that threatens our world, and your strength truly inspires us all. Thank you very much. Thank you. Tonight we pledge to honor Otto's memory with total American resolve. Thank you.

"Finally... we are joined by one more witness to the ominous nature of this regime. His name is Mr. Ji Seong-ho. In 1996, Seong-ho was a starving boy in North Korea. One day, he tried to steal coal from a railroad car to barter for a few scraps of food, which were very hard to get. In the process, he passed out on the train tracks, exhausted from hunger. He woke up as a train ran over his limbs. He then endured multiple amputations without anything to dull the pain or the hurt.

"His brother and sister gave what little food they had to help him recover and ate dirt themselves, permanently stunting their own growth. Later, he was tortured by North Korean authorities after returning from a brief visit to China. His tormentors wanted to know if he'd met any Christians. He had, and he resolved after that to be free.

"Seong-ho traveled thousands of miles on crutches all across China and Southeast Asia to freedom. Most of his family followed. His father was caught trying to escape and was tortured to death. Today he lives in Seoul, where he rescues other defectors, and broadcasts into North Korea what the regime fears most: the truth.

"Today he has a new leg, but Seong-ho, I understand you still keep those old crutches as a reminder of how far you've come. Your great sacrifice is an inspiration to us all. Please. Thank you.

"Seong-ho's story is a testament to the yearning of every human soul to live in freedom. It was that same yearning for freedom that nearly 250 years ago gave birth to a special place called America. It was a small cluster of colonies caught between a great ocean and a vast wilderness. It was home to an incredible people with a revolutionary idea, that they could rule themselves, that they could chart their own destiny, and that, together, they could light up the entire world.

"That is what our country has always been about. That is what Americans have always stood for, always strived for, and always done.

"Atop the dome of this Capitol stands the Statue of Freedom. She stands tall and dignified among the monuments to our ancestors who fought and lived and died to protect her. Monuments to Washington and Jefferson, and Lincoln and King. Memorials to the heroes of Yorktown and Saratoga, to young Americans who shed their blood on the shores of Normandy and the fields beyond. And others who went down in the waters of the Pacific and the skies all over Asia.

"And freedom stands tall over one more monument: this one. This Capitol. This living monument. This is the monument to the American people.

"We're a people whose heroes live not only in the past, but all around us, defending hope, pride, and defending the American way. They work in every trade. They sacrifice to raise a family. They care for our children at home. They defend our flag abroad. And they are strong moms and brave kids. They are firefighters and police officers and border agents, medics and Marines. But above all else, they are Americans. And this Capitol, this city, this Nation belongs entirely to them.

"Our task is to respect them, to listen to them, to serve them, to protect them, and to always be worthy of them. Americans fill the world with art and music. They push the bounds of science and discovery. And they forever remind us of what we should never, ever forget: The people dreamed this country. The people built this country. And it's the people who are making America great again.

"As long as we are proud of who we are and what we are fighting for, there is nothing we cannot achieve.
"As long as we have confidence in our values, faith in our citizens, and trust in our God, we will never fail.
Our families will thrive. Our people will prosper. And our nation will forever be safe and strong and proud and mighty and free.

"Thank you, and God bless America. Good night." (https://bit.ly/2YF12r4)

ASSASSINATION

There is no question that the Deep State/Cabal has wanted to destroy this president.

At this time, April 2020, Attorney General Barr has said there is something deeply troubling about the way the FBI started its effort to sabotage the presidency.

He said criminal charges can be expected, although that would require some time since the issue was spread out over a period of years, starting perhaps as early as 2016.

The FBI lied to the FISA court to get a surveillance warrant on one of Donald Trump's campaign staff, which would have meant they could extend their surveillance right into any phone discussions Trump himself might be engaged in.

And then there was the two-year Mueller witch hunt, as the president often called it. After wasting as much as $45 million dollars, the witch hunters came up empty.

There was no collusion with Russia, which is precisely what President Trump had truthfully said all the way through. Of course, the Cabal News Network (CNN) and their cohorts are unable to recognize truth in any form these days.

Though never reported by the DSM (Deep State Media) at the time President Trump was defusing the potential for nuclear war by meeting with North Korea's Kim Jong Un in Singapore, there was an assassination attempt using a rocket intended to down Air Force One.

It was fired from Puget Sound near Seattle, but an image of the blazing tail of the ascending missile caught on video was quickly debunked as being nothing but a helicopter traveling with its searchlight on.

Having flown in helicopters many times, and once having watched a launch from Cape Canaveral (1977) it was very clear that this debunking was a pre-planned cover-up for what was a real event.

The missile either missed its target, or was locked onto and destroyed with some super-secret weaponry on the fighter jets protecting Air Force On. I produced a video on that assassination attempt for my YouTube channel. If it is still up, you can view it at this link (https://bit.ly/2SIRx6B).

Q wrote about assassinations in his Post 2807 Feb 19 2019. "RETAIN CONTROL vs. LOSE CONTROL. Kennedy was an outsider **[assassinated]**. Reagan was an outsider **[assassination attempt]**. POTUS is an outsider **[CLAS HIGH]**." (CLAS HIGH means Q is not at liberty to reveal any details about what might have occurred – and been foiled.)

Q also used a President John F Kennedy quote in Post 2573, Dec 10 2018. "The times are too grave, the challenge too urgent, and the stakes too high — to permit the customary passions of political debate. We are not here to curse the darkness, but to light the candle that can guide us through that darkness to a safe and sane future."–JFK. Q.

As we know, JFK was publicly assassinated in Dallas Texas in 1963. No thinking person has ever been satisfied with the official inquiry and claim that it was the work of a single gunman.

There is an Internet meme which says "In the three years after the murders of President Kennedy and Lee Harvey Oswald, eighteen material witnesses died... six by gunfire, three in motor accidents, two by suicide, one from a cut throat, one from a karate chop to the neck, three from heart attacks, and two from natural causes."

The organization that masterminded that assassination, and the following attempt on President Reagan's life, is the same deep dark organization that wants to rid the world of President Trump.

Interestingly, where President Kennedy said we are here to light the candle that can lead us through the darkness to the light, President Trump has also recently said "there is light at the end of the tunnel." The metaphor of Dark to Light has frequently been used by Q, and can be found on many Qanon memes.

So once again, an outsider is inside the White House. Hence the full-on nonstop media attacks, failed investigations, failed inquiries and failed impeachment.

By their actions the leaders of the Democrat party, along with many of their subordinate politicians, and even some within the Republican party (e.g. Mitt Romney and formerly John McCain) have shown that without a doubt they are on board with that Dark Agenda.

They want "Orangemanbad" out of there because he is The One (if you recall that term from The Matrix movies) who stands between them and their final goal of global governance.

Again, the president must surely have been aware of all these Black Hat scenarios. He had said during his campaign "I will gladly take all these slings and arrows for you," because it truly has been his intention to Make America Great Again – to once again lift this country to the top tier in world affairs, unfettered by bad treaties and bad deals with other countries.

And that's exactly what he told world leaders at the United Nations in 2018.

2018 UN SPEECH

Speaking to the United Nations on September 25 2018, President Trump again made it very clear where America stands when it comes to globalism.

Following is the transcript of the full speech, included for the record, but also because through careful reading, one can perceive what the man's agenda is, and how much he treasures America's core values.

What he says stands in stark contrast to how he is portrayed by his deadly opponents.

....

Madam President, Mr. Secretary-General, world leaders, ambassadors, and distinguished delegates:

One year ago, I stood before you for the first time in this grand hall. I addressed the threats facing our world, and I presented a vision to achieve a brighter future for all of humanity.

Today, I stand before the United Nations General Assembly to share the extraordinary progress we've made.

In less than two years, my administration has accomplished more than almost any administration in the history of our country.

America's -- so true. [Laughter] Didn't expect that reaction, but that's okay. [Laughter and applause.]

America's economy is booming like never before. Since my election, we've added $10 trillion in wealth. The stock market is at an all-time high in history, and jobless claims are at a 50-year low. African American, Hispanic American, and Asian American unemployment have all achieved their lowest levels ever recorded. We've added more than 4 million new jobs, including half a million manufacturing jobs.

We have passed the biggest tax cuts and reforms in American history. We've started the construction of a major border wall, and we have greatly strengthened border security.

We have secured record funding for our military -- $700 billion this year, and $716 billion next year. Our military will soon be more powerful than it has ever been before.

In other words, the United States is stronger, safer, and a richer country than it was when I assumed office less than two years ago.

We are standing up for America and for the American people. And we are also standing up for the world.

This is great news for our citizens and for peace-loving people everywhere. We believe that when nations respect the rights of their neighbors, and defend the interests of their people, they can better work together to secure the blessings of safety, prosperity, and peace.

Each of us here today is the emissary of a distinct culture, a rich history, and a people bound together by ties of memory, tradition, and the values that make our homelands like nowhere else on Earth.

That is why America will always choose independence and cooperation over global governance, control, and domination.

I honor the right of every nation in this room to pursue its own customs, beliefs, and traditions. The United States will not tell you how to live or work or worship. We only ask that you honor our sovereignty in return.

From Warsaw to Brussels, to Tokyo to Singapore, it has been my highest honor to represent the United States abroad. I have forged close relationships and friendships and strong partnerships with the leaders of many nations in this room, and our approach has already yielded incredible change.

With support from many countries here today, we have engaged with North Korea to replace the specter of conflict with a bold and new push for peace.
In June, I traveled to Singapore to meet face to face with North Korea's leader, Chairman Kim Jong Un. We had highly productive conversations and meetings, and we agreed that it was in both countries' interest to pursue the denuclearization of the Korean Peninsula. Since that meeting, we have already seen a number of encouraging measures that few could have imagined only a short time ago.

The missiles and rockets are no longer flying in every direction. Nuclear testing has stopped. Some military facilities are already being dismantled. Our hostages have been released. And as promised, the remains of our fallen heroes are being returned home to lay at rest in American soil.
I would like to thank Chairman Kim for his courage and for the steps he has taken, though much work remains to be done. The sanctions will stay in place until denuclearization occurs.

I also want to thank the many member states who helped us reach this moment -- a moment that is actually far greater than people would understand; far greater -- but for also their support and the critical support that we will all need going forward.

A special thanks to President Moon of South Korea, Prime Minister Abe of Japan, and President Xi of China.

In the Middle East, our new approach is also yielding great strides and very historic change.

Following my trip to Saudi Arabia last year, the Gulf countries opened a new center to target terrorist financing. They are enforcing new sanctions, working with us to identify and track terrorist networks, and taking more responsibility for fighting terrorism and extremism in their own region.

The UAE, Saudi Arabia, and Qatar have pledged billions of dollars to aid the people of Syria and Yemen. And they are pursuing multiple avenues to ending Yemen's horrible, horrific civil war.

Ultimately, it is up to the nations of the region to decide what kind of future they want for themselves and their children.

For that reason, the United States is working with the Gulf Cooperation Council, Jordan, and Egypt to establish a regional strategic alliance so that Middle Eastern nations can advance prosperity, stability, and security across their home region.

Thanks to the United States military and our partnership with many of your nations, I am pleased to report that the bloodthirsty killers known as ISIS have been driven out from the territory they once held in Iraq and Syria. We will continue to work with friends and allies to deny radical Islamic terrorists any funding, territory or support, or any means of infiltrating

our borders.
The ongoing tragedy in Syria is heartbreaking.

Our shared goals must be the de-escalation of military conflict, along with a political solution that honors the will of the Syrian people. In this vein, we urge the United Nations-led peace process be reinvigorated. But, rest assured, the United States will respond if chemical weapons are deployed by the Assad regime.

I commend the people of Jordan and other neighboring countries for hosting refugees from this very brutal civil war.

As we see in Jordan, the most compassionate policy is to place refugees as close to their homes as possible to ease their eventual return to be part of the rebuilding process. This approach also stretches finite resources to help far more people, increasing the impact of every dollar spent.

Every solution to the humanitarian crisis in Syria must also include a strategy to address the brutal regime that has fueled and financed it: the corrupt dictatorship in Iran.

Iran's leaders sow chaos, death, and destruction. They do not respect their neighbors or borders, or the sovereign rights of nations. Instead, Iran's leaders plunder the nation's resources to enrich themselves and to spread mayhem across the Middle East and far beyond.

The Iranian people are rightly outraged that their leaders have embezzled billions of dollars from Iran's treasury, seized valuable portions of the economy, and looted the people's religious endowments, all to line their own pockets and send their proxies to wage war. Not good.

Iran's neighbors have paid a heavy toll for the region's [regime's] agenda of aggression and expansion. That is why so many countries in the Middle East strongly supported my decision to withdraw the United States from the horrible 2015 Iran Nuclear Deal and re-impose nuclear sanctions.

The Iran deal was a windfall for Iran's leaders. In the years since the deal was reached, Iran's military budget grew nearly 40 percent. The dictatorship used the funds to build nuclear-capable missiles, increase internal repression, finance terrorism, and fund havoc and slaughter in Syria and Yemen.

The United States has launched a campaign of economic pressure to deny the regime the funds it needs to advance its bloody agenda. Last month, we began re-imposing hard-hitting nuclear sanctions that had been lifted under the Iran deal. Additional sanctions will resume November 5th, and more will follow. And we're working with countries that import Iranian crude oil to cut their purchases substantially.

We cannot allow the world's leading sponsor of terrorism to possess the planet's most dangerous weapons. We cannot allow a regime that chants "Death to America," and that threatens Israel with annihilation, to possess the means to deliver a nuclear warhead to any city on Earth. Just can't do it.

We ask all nations to isolate Iran's regime as long as its aggression continues. And we ask all nations to support Iran's people as they struggle to reclaim their religious and righteous destiny.

This year, we also took another significant step forward in the Middle East. In recognition of every sovereign state to determine its own capital, I moved the U.S. Embassy in Israel to Jerusalem.

The United States is committed to a future of peace and stability in the region, including peace between the Israelis and the Palestinians. That aim is advanced, not harmed, by acknowledging the obvious facts.

America's policy of principled realism means we will not be held hostage to old dogmas, discredited ideologies, and so-called experts who have been proven wrong over the years, time and time again. This is true not only in matters of peace, but in matters of prosperity.

We believe that trade must be fair and reciprocal. The United States will not be taken advantage of any longer.

For decades, the United States opened its economy -- the largest, by far, on Earth -- with few conditions. We allowed foreign goods from all over the world to flow freely across our borders.

Yet, other countries did not grant us fair and reciprocal access to their markets in return. Even worse, some countries abused their openness to dump their products, subsidize their goods, target our industries, and manipulate their currencies to gain unfair advantage over our country. As a result, our trade deficit ballooned to nearly $800 billion a year.

For this reason, we are systematically renegotiating broken and bad trade deals.

Last month, we announced a groundbreaking U.S.-Mexico trade agreement. And just yesterday, I stood with President Moon to announce the successful completion of the brand new U.S.-Korea trade deal. And this is just the beginning.

Many nations in this hall will agree that the world trading system is in dire need of change. For example, countries were admitted to the World Trade Organization that violate every single principle on which the organization is based. While the United States and many other nations play by the rules, these countries use government-run industrial planning and state-owned enterprises to rig the system in their favor. They engage in relentless product dumping, forced technology transfer, and the theft of intellectual property.

The United States lost over 3 million manufacturing jobs, nearly a quarter of all steel jobs, and 60,000 factories after China joined the WTO. And we have racked up $13 trillion in trade deficits over the last two decades.

But those days are over. We will no longer tolerate such abuse. We will not allow our workers to be victimized, our companies to be cheated, and our wealth to be plundered and transferred. America will never apologize for protecting its citizens.

The United States has just announced tariffs on another $200 billion in Chinese-made goods for a total, so far, of $250 billion. I have great respect and affection for my friend, President Xi, but I have made clear our trade imbalance is just not acceptable. China's market distortions and the way they deal cannot be tolerated.

As my administration has demonstrated, America will always act in our national interest.

I spoke before this body last year and warned that the U.N. Human Rights Council had become a grave embarrassment to this institution, shielding egregious human rights abusers while bashing America and its many friends.

Our Ambassador to the United Nations, Nikki Haley, laid out a clear agenda for reform, but despite reported and repeated warnings, no action at all was taken. So the United States took the only responsible course: We withdrew from the Human Rights Council, and we will not return until real reform is enacted.

For similar reasons, the United States will provide no support in recognition to the International Criminal Court. As far as America is concerned, the ICC has no jurisdiction, no legitimacy, and no authority. The ICC claims near-universal jurisdiction over the citizens of every country, violating all principles of justice, fairness, and due process. We will never surrender America's sovereignty to an unelected, unaccountable, global bureaucracy.

America is governed by Americans. We reject the ideology of globalism, and we embrace the doctrine of patriotism.

Around the world, responsible nations must defend against threats to sovereignty not just from global governance, but also from other, new forms of coercion and domination.

In America, we believe strongly in energy security for ourselves and for our allies. We have become the largest energy producer anywhere on the face of the Earth. The United States stands ready to export our abundant, affordable supply of oil, clean coal, and natural gas.

OPEC and OPEC nations, are, as usual, ripping off the rest of the world, and I don't like it. Nobody should like it. We defend many of these nations for nothing, and then they take advantage of us by giving us high oil prices. Not good.
We want them to stop raising prices, we want them to start lowering prices, and they must contribute substantially to military protection from now on. We are not going to put up with it -- these horrible prices -- much longer.

Reliance on a single foreign supplier can leave a nation vulnerable to extortion and intimidation. That is why we congratulate European states, such as Poland, for leading the construction of a Baltic pipeline so that nations are not dependent on Russia to meet their energy needs. Germany will become totally dependent on Russian energy if it does not immediately change course.

Here in the Western Hemisphere, we are committed to maintaining our independence from the encroachment of expansionist foreign powers.

t has been the formal policy of our country since President Monroe that we reject the interference of foreign nations in this hemisphere and in our own affairs. The United States has recently strengthened our laws to better screen foreign investments in our country for national security threats, and we welcome cooperation with countries in this region and around the world that wish to do the same. You need to do it for your own protection.

The United States is also working with partners in Latin America to confront threats to sovereignty from uncontrolled migration. Tolerance for human struggling and human smuggling and trafficking is not humane. It's a horrible thing that's going on, at levels that nobody has ever seen before. It's very, very cruel.

Illegal immigration funds criminal networks, ruthless gangs, and the flow of deadly drugs. Illegal immigration exploits vulnerable populations, hurts hardworking citizens, and has produced a vicious cycle of crime, violence, and poverty. Only by upholding national borders, destroying criminal gangs, can we break this cycle and establish a real foundation for prosperity.

We recognize the right of every nation in this room to set its own immigration policy in accordance with its national interests, just as we ask other countries to respect our own right to do the same -- which we are doing. That is one reason the United States will not participate in the new Global Compact on Migration. Migration should not be governed by an international body unaccountable to our own citizens.

Ultimately, the only long-term solution to the migration crisis is to help people build more hopeful futures in their home countries. Make their countries great again.

Currently, we are witnessing a human tragedy, as an example, in Venezuela. More than 2 million people have fled the anguish inflicted by the socialist Maduro regime and its Cuban sponsors.

Not long ago, Venezuela was one of the richest countries on Earth. Today, socialism has bankrupted the oil-rich nation and driven its people into abject poverty.

Virtually everywhere socialism or communism has been tried, it has produced suffering, corruption, and decay. Socialism's thirst for power leads to expansion, incursion, and oppression. All nations of the world should resist socialism and the misery that it brings to everyone.

In that spirit, we ask the nations gathered here to join us in calling for the restoration of democracy in Venezuela. Today, we are announcing additional sanctions against the repressive regime, targeting Maduro's inner circle and close advisors.

We are grateful for all the work the United Nations does around the world to help people build better lives for themselves and their families.

The United States is the world's largest giver in the world, by far, of foreign aid. But few give anything to us. That is why we are taking a hard look at U.S. foreign assistance. That will be headed up by Secretary of State Mike Pompeo. We will examine what is working, what is not working, and whether the countries who receive our dollars and our protection also have our interests at heart.

Moving forward, we are only going to give foreign aid to those who respect us and, frankly, are our friends. And we expect other countries to pay their fair share for the cost of their defense.

The United States is committed to making the United Nations more effective and accountable. I have said many times that the United Nations has unlimited potential. As part of our reform effort, I have told our negotiators that the United States will not pay more than 25 percent of the U.N. peacekeeping budget. This will encourage other countries to step up, get involved, and also share in this very large burden.

And we are working to shift more of our funding from assessed contributions to voluntary so that we can target American resources to the programs with the best record of success.

Only when each of us does our part and contributes our share can we realize the U.N.'s highest aspirations. We must pursue peace without fear, hope without despair, and security without apology.

Looking around this hall where so much history has transpired, we think of the many before us who have come here to address the challenges of their nations and of their times. And our thoughts turn to the same question that ran through all their speeches and resolutions, through every word and every hope. It is the question of what kind of world will we leave for our children and what kind of nations they will inherit.

The dreams that fill this hall today are as diverse as the people who have stood at this podium, and as varied as the countries represented right here in this body are. It really is something. It really is great, great history.
There is India, a free society over a billion people, successfully lifting countless millions out of poverty and into the middle

class.

There is Saudi Arabia, where King Salman and the Crown Prince are pursuing bold new reforms.

There is Israel, proudly celebrating its 70th anniversary as a thriving democracy in the Holy Land.

In Poland, a great people are standing up for their independence, their security, and their sovereignty.

Many countries are pursuing their own unique visions, building their own hopeful futures, and chasing their own wonderful dreams of destiny, of legacy, and of a home.

The whole world is richer, humanity is better, because of this beautiful constellation of nations, each very special, each very unique, and each shining brightly in its part of the world.

In each one, we see awesome promise of a people bound together by a shared past and working toward a common future.

As for Americans, we know what kind of future we want for ourselves. We know what kind of a nation America must always be.

In America, we believe in the majesty of freedom and the dignity of the individual. We believe in self-government and the rule of law. And we prize the culture that sustains our liberty — a culture built on strong families, deep faith, and fierce independence. We celebrate our heroes, we treasure our traditions, and above all, we love our country.

Inside everyone in this great chamber today, and everyone listening all around the globe, there is the heart of a patriot that feels the same powerful love for your nation, the same intense loyalty to your homeland.

The passion that burns in the hearts of patriots and the souls of nations has inspired reform and revolution, sacrifice and selflessness, scientific breakthroughs, and magnificent works of art.

Our task is not to erase it, but to embrace it. To build with it. To draw on its ancient wisdom. And to find within it the will to make our nations greater, our regions safer, and the world better.

To unleash this incredible potential in our people, we must defend the foundations that make it all possible. Sovereign and independent nations are the only vehicle where freedom has ever survived, democracy has ever endured, or peace has ever prospered. And so we must protect our sovereignty and our cherished independence above all.

When we do, we will find new avenues for cooperation unfolding before us. We will find new passion for peacemaking rising within us. We will find new purpose, new resolve, and new spirit flourishing all around us, and making this a more beautiful world in which to live.

So together, let us choose a future of patriotism, prosperity, and pride. Let us choose peace and freedom over domination and defeat. And let us come here to this place to stand for our people and their nations, forever strong, forever sovereign, forever just, and forever thankful for the grace and the goodness and the glory of God.

Thank you. God bless you. And God bless the nations of the world. Thank you very much. Thank you.

ABOUT TRUMP

As I was putting the final touches to this book, I received an email from a subscriber to my North Star News newsletter containing a link to orientalreview.org and an article headed "About Trump."

The following essay is reprinted with permission as per a footnote to the article, "Reposts are welcomed with the reference to ORIENTAL REVIEW." (https://orientalreview.org/2019/11/15/about-trump/)

In some of my YouTube videos I have referred to President Trump as a 3D chess player, always many moves ahead of his opponents.

This article, published in November 2019, had had over 146,000 views by early June 2020. It takes the chess metaphor to the next level.

....

Written by Sylvain LAFOREST on 15/11/2019

The timing is right for everyone to understand what Donald Trump is doing, and try to decrypt the ambiguity of how he is doing it.
The controversial President has a much clearer agenda than anyone can imagine on both foreign policy and internal affairs, but since he has to stay in power or even stay alive to achieve his objectives, his strategy is so refined and subtle that next to no one can see it.

His overall objective is so ambitious that he has to follow random elliptic courses to get from point A to point B, using patterns that throw people off on their comprehension of the man.

That includes most independent journalists and so-called alternative analysts, as much as Western mainstream fake-news publishers and a large majority of the population.

To start off, let's clear the one aspect of his mission that is straightforward and terribly direct: he's the first and only American President to ever address humanity's worst collective flaw, its total ignorance of reality.

Because medias and education are both controlled by the handful of billionaires that are running the planet, we don't know anything about our history that's been twisted dry by the winners, and we don't have a clue about our present world.

As he stepped in the political arena, Donald popularized the expression «fake news» to convince the American citizens, and the world population as well, that medias always lie to you.

The expression has now become commonplace, but do you realize how deeply shocking is the fact that nearly everything you think you know is totally fake? Media lies don't just cover history and politics, but they have shaped your false perception on topics like economy, food, climate, health, on everything.

What if I told you that we know exactly who shot JFK from the grassy knoll, that the foreknowledge of Pearl Harbor was proven in court, that the $CO2$ greenhouse effect is scientifically absurd, that our money is created through loans by banks who don't even have the funds, or that science proves with a 100% certainty that 911 was an inside job?

Ever heard of a mainstream journalist, PBS documentary or university teacher telling you about any of this? 44 Presidents came and went without even raising one word about this huge problem, before the 45th came along.

Trump knows that freeing the people out of this unfathomable ignorance is the first step to overall freedom, so he started calling mainstream journalists and their news outlets for what they are: pathological liars.

> «Thousands of mental health professionals agree with Woodward and the New York Times op-ed author: Trump is dangerous.» – **Bandy X. Lee, The Conversation 2018**

> «The question is not whether the President is crazy but whether he is crazy like a fox or crazy like crazy.» – **Masha Gessen, The New Yorker 2017**

Let's make one thing clear: to the establishment, Trump isn't mentally challenged, but he's definitely seen as a possible nemesis of their world.

Ever since he moved in the White House, Trump has been depicted as a narcissist, a racist, a sexist and a climate-skeptic, loaded with shady past stories and mental issues.

Even though an approximate 60% of the American people don't trust medias anymore, many have bought the story that Trump might be slightly crazy or unfit to rule, and the statistic climbs even higher when you get out of the USA.

Of course, Donald isn't doing anything special to change the deeply negative perception that so many journalists and people alike have about him.

He's openly outrageous and provocative on Twitter, he sounds impulsive and dumb most of the time, acts irrationally, lies on a daily basis, and throws out sanctions and threats as if they were candy canes out of an elf's side bag in a mall in December.

Right away, we can destroy one persistent media myth: the image Trump is projecting is self-destructive and it's the exact opposite of how pathological narcissists act, since they thrive to be loved and admired by everyone. Donald simply doesn't care if you like him or not, which makes him the ultimate anti-narcissist, by its psychological definition. And that's not even up for opinion, it's a quite simple and undeniable fact.

His general plan exhales from one of his favorite motto: «We will give power back to the people», because the United States and its imperialist web woven over the world have been in the hands of a few globalist bankers, military industrials and multinationals for more than a century.

To achieve his plan, he has to end wars abroad, bring back the kids, dismantle the NATO and CIA, get control over the Federal Reserve, cut every link with foreign allies, abolish the Swift financial system, demolish the propaganda power of the medias, drain the swamp of the deep state that's running the spying agencies and disable the shadow government that's lurking in the Council on foreign relations and Trilateral Commission's offices.

In short, he has to destroy the New World Order and its globalist ideology. The task is huge and dangerous to say the least. Thankfully, he's not alone.

Before we get on his techniques and tactics, we have to know a little bit more about what's really been going on in the world.

Mighty Russia

Since Peter the Great, the whole history of Russia is a permanent demonstration of its will to maintain its political and economical independence from international banks and imperialism, pushing this great nation to help many smaller countries fighting to keep their own independence.

Twice Russia helped the United States against the British/Rothschild Empire; first by openly supporting them in the Independence War, and again in the Civil War, when Rothschild's were funding the Confederates to politically break down the nation to bring it back in the British colonial Empire's coop.

Russia also destroyed Napoleon and the Nazis, whom were both funded by international banks as tools to crush economically independent nations.

Independence is in their DNA. After almost a decade of Western oligarchy taking over Russia's economy after the fall of USSR in 1991, Putin took power and drained the Russian swamp.

Since then, each and every move that he has made aims to destroy the American Empire, or the entity that replaced the British Empire in 1944, which is the non-conspiracy theory name of the New World Order.

The new empire is basically the same central banking scheme, with just a slightly different set of owners that switched the British army for NATO, as their world Gestapo.

Until Trump came along, Putin was single handedly fighting the New World Order who's century-old obsession is the control of the world oil market, since oil is the blood running through the veins of the world economy. Oil is a thousand times more valuable than gold.

Cargo ships, airplanes and armies don't run on batteries. Therefore, to counter the globalists, Putin developed the best offensive and defensive missile systems, with the result that Russia can now protect every independent oil producer such as Syria, Venezuela and Iran.

Central bankers and the US shadow government are still hanging on to their dying plan, because without a victory in Syria, there's no enlarging Israel, thus ending the century-old fantasy of uniting the Middle East oil production in the hands of the New World Order. Ask Lord Balfour if you have any doubt. That's the real stake of the Syrian war, it's nothing short of do or die.

A century of lies

Now, because a shadow government is giving direct orders to the CIA and NATO in the name of banks and industries, Trump has no control over the military.

The deep state is a rosary of permanent officials ruling Washington and the Pentagon, that only respond to their orders. If you still believe that the «Commander in chief» is in charge, explain why every time Trump ordered to pull out of Syria and Afghanistan, more troops came in?

As I'm writing this text, US and NATO troops pulled out of the Kurdish zones, went to Iraq, and came back with heavier equipment around the oil reserves of Syria.
Donald has a lot more of swamp draining to do before the Pentagon actually listens to anything he says.

Trump should be outraged and denunciate out loud that the military command doesn't bother about what he thinks, but this would ignite an unimaginable chaos, and perhaps even a civil war in the US, if the citizens who own roughly 393 million weapons in their homes were to learn that private interests are in charge of the military.

It would also lead to a very simple but dramatic question: «What is exactly the purpose of democracy?» These weapons are the titanium fences guarding the population from a totalitarian Big Brother.

One has to realize how much trouble the US army and spying agencies have been going through in creating false-flag operations for more than a century, so that their interventions always looked righteous, in the name of democracy promotion, human rights and justice around the planet.

They blew up the Maine ship in 1898 to enter the Hispanic-American war, then the Lusitania in 1915 to enter WW1. They pushed Japan to attack Pearl Harbor in 1941, knew about the attack 10 days in advance and said nothing to the Hawaiian base. They made up a North Vietnamese torpedo aggression on their ships in the Tonkin Bay to justify sending boots on the Vietnamese ground.

They made up a story of Iraqi soldiers destroying nurseries to invade Kuwait in 1991. They invented mass destruction weapons to attack Iraq again in 2003, and organized 911 to shred the 1789 Constitution, attack Afghanistan and launch a War on terror.

This totally fake mask of virtue has to be preserved for controlling the opinion of the American citizens and their domestic arsenal, who have to believe that they wear the white cowboy hats of democracy.

So how did Trump react when he learned that American troops were re-entering Syria? He repeated again and again in every interview and declaration that «we have secured the oil fields of Syria», and even added «I'm thinking about sending Exxon in the region to take care of the Syrian oil».

Neocons, Zionists and banks were thrilled, but everyone else is outraged, because the vast majority doesn't understand that Trump is swallowing this pill solely for its after-effects.

On this single bottle is written in fine print that «the use of this drug might force American-NATO troops out of Syria under the pressure of the united world community and flabbergasted American population.»

Trump made the situation unsustainable for NATO to stay in Syria, and how he's been repeating this deeply shocking, politically incorrect position clearly shows his real intention. He destroyed over a century of fake virtue in a single sentence.

Trump is a historical anomaly

Trump is only the fourth president in US history to actually fight for the people, unlike all 41 others, who mainly channeled the people's money in a pipeline of dollars that ends up in private banks.

First there was Andrew Jackson who was shot after he destroyed the Second National Bank that he openly accused of being controlled by the Rothschild and The City in London.

Then there was Abraham Lincoln, who was murdered after printing his «greenbacks», national money that the state issued to pay the soldiers because Lincoln had refused to borrow money from Rothschild at 24% interest.

Then there was JFK, who was killed for a dozen reasons that mostly went against the banks and military industries profits, and now is Donald Trump, who shouted that he would «Give America back to the people».

Like most businessmen, Trump hates banks, for the formidable power that they have over the economy. Just take a peek at Henry Ford's only book, «The International Jew» to find out how deep was his distrust and hatred of international banks.

Trump's businesses have suffered a lot because of these institutions that basically sell you an umbrella, only to take it back as soon as it rains.

Private banking's control over money creation and interest rates, through every Central Bank of almost every country is a permanent power over nations, far above the ephemeral cycle of politicians.

By the year 2000, these nation looters were only a few steps away from their planetary totalitarian dream, but a couple of details stood still: Vladimir Putin and 393 million American weapons.

Then came along orange-faced Donald, the last piece in the puzzle that we the people, needed to terminate 250 years of the banking empire.

Techniques and tactics

Early in his mandate, Trump naively tried the direct approach, by surrounding himself with establishment rebels like Michael Flynn and Steve Bannon, then by annoying each and everyone of his foreign allies, shredding their free-trade treaties, imposing taxes on imports and insulting them in their face in the G7 meetings of 2017 and 2018.

The reaction was strong and everyone doubled-down on the Russiagate absurdity, as it looked like the only option to stop the man on his path of globalism destruction.

Predictably, the direct approach went nowhere; Flynn and Bannon had to go, and Trump was entangled in a handful of inquiries that made him realize that he wouldn't get anything accomplished with transparency.

He had to find a way to annihilate the most dangerous people on the planet, but at the same time, stay in power and alive. He had to smarten up.

That's when his genius exploded on the world. He completely changed his strategy and approach, and started taking absurd decisions and tweeting outrageous declarations.

As threatening and dangerous as some of these first looked, Trump didn't use them for their first degree meaning, but was aiming at the genuine second degree effects that his moves would have. And he didn't care about what people thought of him as he did, for only results count in the end.

 He would even play buffoon over Twitter, look naive, lunatic or downright idiotic, perhaps in the hope to impregnate the belief that he didn't know what he's doing, and that he couldn't be that dangerous.

He's willfully being politically incorrect to show the ugly face that the United States are hiding behind their mask.

The first test on his new approach was to try to stop the growing danger of an attack and invasion of North Korea by NATO. Trump insulted Kim Jung-Un through Twitter, called him Rocket Man, and threatened to nuke North Korea to the ground.

His raging political incorrectness went on for weeks until it sank in everyone's minds that those were not good reasons to attack a country. He paralyzed NATO.

Trump then met Rocket Man, and they walked in the park with the start of a beautiful friendship, laughing together, while accomplishing absolutely nothing in their negotiations, since they have nothing to negotiate about.

Many were talking about the Nobel price for peace, because many don't know that it's usually handed to whitewash war criminals like Obama or Kissinger.

Then came Venezuela. Trump pushed his tactic a step further, to make sure that no one could support an attack on the free country.

He put the worst neo-cons available on the case: Elliott Abrams, formerly convicted of conspiracy in the Iran-Contras deal in the '80s and John Bolton, famous first-degree warmonger.

Trump then confirmed Juan Guaido as his choice for president of Venezuela; an empty puppet so dumb that he can't even see how much he's being used.

Again, Trump threatened to burn the country to rubbles, while the world community watched in awe the total lack of subtlety and diplomacy in Trump's behavior, with the result that Brazil and Colombia backed away and said they wanted nothing to do with an attack on Venezuela.

Trump's medicine left only 40 satellite countries worldwide, with Presidents and Prime Ministers brain dead enough to shyly support Guaido the Jester. Donald checked the box beside Venezuela on his list and kept scrolling down.

Then came the two gifts to Israel: Jerusalem as a capital, and the Syrian Golan Heights as its confirmed possession. Netanyahu whom isn't the sharpest pencil in the box jumped of joy, and everyone yelled that Trump was a Zionist.

The real after-effect result was that the whole of the Middle East united against Israel, which no one can support anymore.

Even their historical accomplice Saudi Arabia had to openly disapprove this huge slap in the face of Islam. The two Trump gifts were in fact back stabs in the Israel state, whose future doesn't look too bright nowadays, since NATO will have to move out of the region. Check again.

As reality sinks in

But there's more! With his lack of control over NATO and the army, Trump is very limited in his actions.

At first glance, the outstanding multiplication of economical sanctions on countries like Russia, Turkey, China, Iran, Venezuela and other nations look tough and merciless, but the reality of these sanctions pushed those countries out of the Swift financial system designed to keep enslaving nations through the dollar hegemony, and they're all slipping away from the international banks' grip.

It forced Russia, China and India to create an alternative system of trade payments based on national currencies, instead of the almighty dollar.

The bipolar reality of the world is now official, and with his upcoming next sanctions, Trump will push more countries out of the Swift system to join the other side, while important banks are starting to fall in Europe.

Even in the political hurricane Trump is in, he still finds time to display his almost childish arrogant humor.

Look at his grandiose mockery of Hillary Clinton and Barrack

Obama, as he sat down with the most straight-faced generals he could find, to take a picture in a so-called «situation room» as they faked the monitoring of the death of Baghdadi somewhere he couldn't be, exactly like his criminal predecessors did a long time ago with the fake Bin Laden killing.

He even pushed the farce to adding the details of a dog recognizing Daesch's fake caliph by sniffing his underwear. Now that you understand what Trump is really about, you will also be able to appreciate the show, in all of its splendor and true meaning."

«We have secured the oil fields of Syria». Indeed, with this short sentence, Trump joined his voice to that of General Smedley Butler who rocked the world 80 years ago with a tiny book called «War is a racket». Looting and stealing oil is definitely not as virtuous as promoting democracy and justice.

What amazes me is those numerous «alternative» journalists and analysts, who know on the tip of their fingers every technical problem about 911, or scientific reality on the absurd global warming story, but still don't have a clue about what Trump is doing, 3 years in his mandate, because they bought the mainstream media that convinced everyone that Trump is mentally challenged.

For those who still entertain doubts about Trump's agenda, do you really believe that the obvious implosion of American Imperialism over the planet is a coincidence?

Do you still believe that its because of the Russian influence on the 2016 election that the CIA, the FBI, every media, the American Congress, the Federal Reserve, the Democratic party and the warmongering half of the Republicans are working against him and are even trying to impeach him?

Like most stuff that comes out of medias, reality is the exact opposite of what you're being told: Trump might be the most dedicated man to ever set foot in the Oval office. And certainly the most ambitious and politically incorrect.

Conclusion

The world will change drastically between 2020 and 2024. Trump's second and last mandate coincides with Putin's last mandate as President of Russia.

There may never be another coincidence like this for a long time, and both know that it's now or perhaps never. Together, they have to end NATO, Swift, and the European Union should crumble.

Terrorism and anthropogenic global warming will jump in the vortex and disappear with their creators. Trump will have to drain the swamp in the CIA and Pentagon, and he has to nationalize the Federal Reserve.

Along with Xi and Modi, they could put a final end to private banking in public affairs, by refusing to pay a single penny of their debts, and reset the world economy by shifting to national currencies produced by governments, as private banks will fall like dominos, with no more Obama-like servant to bail them out at your expense.

Once this is done, unbearable peace and prosperity could roam the planet, as our taxes pay for the development of our countries instead of buying useless military gear and paying interests on loans by bankers who didn't even have the money in the first place.

If you still don't understand Donald Trump after reading the above, you're hopeless. Or you're might be Trudeau, Macron, Guaido, or any other useful idiot, unaware that the carpet under your feet has already slipped away.

(Reposts are welcomed with the reference to ORIENTAL REVIEW).

About orientalreview.org. Oriental Review "is an international e-journal focusing on current political issues in Eurasia and beyond. The initiative is (sic) launched in February 2010 by a group of freelance bloggers and political analysts concerned with the aggravating security situation in the world.

"Our mission, but (sic) sharing alternative outlooks and providing new edge analysis of the situation in the global 'hot spots', will be in developing the project into a full-fledged Open Dialogue Research Centre.

"We are not affiliated with any particular research institution, foundation or political party. "

Note:- Having reviewed a number of articles by orientalreview's many contributors, I highly recommend it as a research source. For instance, articles include headlines such as "Putin And Trump vs The New World Order: The Final Battle," and "Bill Gates, Vaccinations, Microchips, and Patent 060606," and "The Coronavirus and Hybrid Warfare." Their Home Page is at this link (https://orientalreview.org/)

RESEARCH 101

From here on we're taking a serious look at the art of research.

In preceding chapters I have taken us through a number of research scenarios, the purpose of research being to find for ourselves answers to questions we have on any given subject.

However, it must be said that there really are no final or definitive answers.

That's because every subject is somewhat of a moving target. Information is not static. It is evolving and changing every day, if not every minute.

The floor of the Stock Exchange comes to mind as a visual in that regard. Stock prices can be fluctuating by the second in that super-casino where buyers and sellers are figuratively rolling the dice

The focus of this book has been to learn about the Globalist agenda, and to that end the contents of the Toronto Protocols are, to say the least, chilling. Nevertheless, as shocking as they might be, the very fact that they have been exposed to the light means in a sense that the spread of this awareness plays a major part in putting an end to the Dark Agenda.

"Know they enemy" is so important when it comes to a battle of any sort, and as Q has often said, "the silent war continues."

Personal research is one of the best weapons we can use, because when it comes right down to it, if we are ignorant of the enemy's plans and strategies, we really are susceptible to being controlled, manipulated, herded and fleeced.

Truly, that has been going on for a very long time, and some of us are tired of it. In fact, was it not the control of their lives by emperors and kings and the Upper Class that saw the founders of this nation leave Europe by the thousands?

Even then, it took decades for enough people – and it was only a small percentage of them – to reach the point that it was time for a revolution, and so, thanks to them, the United States of America, a republic akin to that of early Greece under the Archon Solon, came into being.

So too did the Constitution – and that itself should be a subject of personal research once again. Why? Because while we are taught that America truly won its independence from England, we now know that the Rothschilds, as per that statement by Nathan Rothschild, controlled the British Empire. Therefore, the king and so-called Royalty were and are but a front for the Illuminati, the Globalists, the Cabal. They and the Rothschilds and the associated elite families did not give up their goal of world domination just because America went its own way.

Instead, as Q notes quite frequently these days, they began a process of infiltration. They had Lincoln assassinated, and we know the rest of the story – up till now. Or do we? No, we only know what our past (controlled) education has taught us. If we want to know more, we have to research more.

But we have to control ourselves in the process, because it is possible to actually become "over-focused."

To be over-focused means that you're more focused on what's

going on in your head, your own emotions, your own preconceptions than what is in front of your eyes. In researching the chapter "Spies For China" I was so focused on validating my assumption that these three people were most likely a cell of spies for China that had been busted by the FBI, that I initially missed the obvious.

They were *separate* arrests. Hence the additional research into each of those three people, and the discovery that one of them was obviously a spy for the communist Chinese military, the second Chinese national was trying to smuggle some 20 vials of an unnamed virus to China, and Lieber himself was on communist China's payroll.
One might suspect those vials contained some variant of the coronavirus, but that's a suspicion that unfortunately cannot be confirmed. Beyond saying that it appears unusual for the DOJ to have lumped all three into the same press release, albeit with the caveat that they were separate charges, the nagging suspicion that they are related in some way remains.

The best one can do with that is to consider it as a possibility which may be revealed, one way or the other, in the following court cases.

But don't hold your breath for the DSM to report that in any detail. After all, their research only extends to what's inside their heads, and it's all "Orangemanbad."

I'm sure we all have acquaintances who get all their news from the legacy (failing) media and believe everything they're told, then pass on the "juicy bits" as gossip to their like-minded friends and workmates, who in turn pass it on as if it's the gospel truth.

Such was the case with the recent fake news claim that the president had recommended that people inject or imbibe some sort of bleach to combat the virus.

A woman somewhere said she and her husband took fish tank cleaner as a result, and she blamed President Trump for her husband's death.

That made juicy headlines in the DSM, but a week or so later, Qanon researchers on Twitter revealed that she had actually poisoned her husband, had been charged with homicide, and tried to avoid arrest by blaming the president. Lesson: Nothing is as it seems. *There's always more to the story.*

Maybe the president did use the word "inject" when he was asking whether it was possible to "inject" something into the lungs to aid recovery. Maybe he should have said "insert" rather than "inject," and any reporter worth the name would have asked for clarification right then and there.

Interestingly, it turns out that a Colorado company has developed an insertable device containing LED bulbs that emit Ultraviolet light, which in turn has been shown to kill viruses. The president probably already knew that, but he seems to have a way of misusing words, even misspelling them on Twitter, and the media jumps on these apparent slip-ups like flies on stink.

Personally, I think he does those things deliberately, knowing the media will respond as they do, which in turn means they finish up reporting what he wants the wider public to be aware of. Does that seem odd? Of course it does, but he seems to understand that negative press can be just as useful as positive coverage.

For instance, the DSM spends an inordinate amount of time running negative stories about the "Qanon conspiracy theory." What has that done? As Q has frequently said, "these people are stupid." Their coverage, as negative as it might be, has nevertheless had the effect of actually attracting millions of free-thinking people to the Qanon research sites on the Internet.

It doesn't take much research to get a handle on what the Deep State strategy really is. It is all about using any means possible to destroy the president, regardless of how that might affect the US economy. They care nothing for the people of this world.

They do not lose any sleep at all over the fact that the whole planet is in lockdown, millions out of work, economies shattered around the globe, food shortages on the horizon, and mounting protests and demonstrations all over the world.

Having failed to assassinate President Trump in the physical sense, they desperately hope to assassinate his character, his tremendous progress in making America great again, and his chances of being re-elected.

Good research means you look at a set of related circumstances as if they are scattered and apparently disconnected pieces of a big puzzle. Then you do your best to see where and how they fit together. "Connecting the dots" is another metaphor.

The Toronto Protocols, the big reveal about the Illuminati game plan, the Rockefeller Foundation's future scenarios report, Bill Gates touting vaccines for everyone, all these are puzzle pieces. Add to that a timeline of events starting when Donald Trump came down the stairs with his wife to announce that he had decided to run for the presidency.

Against all odds he won the Republican Party nomination. Against all odds he was elected – despite a concerted media campaign that constantly portrayed him as the underdog with their falsified polls and negative articles.

Deep State individuals, and that means from Obama on down,

unlawfully set up the witch hunt that would mutate into the Mueller investigation.

On and on it goes, and he has weathered it all – notably saying shortly after his election, "this is the calm before the storm." Questioned as to "what storm?" he responded, "you'll find out."

How right he was. The storm is upon us. But as one of the many Qanon memes has him saying, "it's you they're after. I'm just in the way." How true that is.

Yet he has been the one around whom the storm has raged for a full four years, amazingly showing no signs of buckling, while in just the past year or two, the Qanon "conspiracy theory" has literally attracted millions worldwide.

It's enough to make you think that there's never been anything like this in the history of this civilization. It's as if we are literally at a crossroads.

One road leads to a dark future and control of the cattle by the New World Order overlords. The other – to the demise of those overlords, and a world of true peace and prosperity.

Importantly though, it's not something to just sit back and dream about and let the president carry the ball and suffer all the brutal knockdowns. If we get into the habit of questioning everything the mainstream media reports, researching everything Trump's opponents do to undermine him (which means undermining America itself) then we are fit to help others should they have questions that they too are concerned about.

Surely, like the Founding Fathers and the men and women of the time, what we all want and deserve is an ongoing life of liberty and the pursuit of happiness.

Happiness does not come from being subservient to the likes of the Cabal and their cohorts. It comes from being a sovereign individual, self reliant, patriotic, and prepared to self-educate so we can see, objectively, what's in front of our eyes.

Only with knowledge and an open mind can we be prepared to do what we must to preserve "the land of the free, because of the brave."
It is time to be brave.
Our future depends on it.

TOP SITES

These suggestions relate specifically to sites and civilian reporters that I have found to be exceptionally useful in my quest to solve the puzzle that is now known by Qanons to be a silent war between Good and Evil, or Dark and Light.

My personal research these days is very much related to what can be found on the various sites that carry Q's posts.

I also hover around Twitter to see what Qanons are saying about current events, and I subscribe to a number of newsletters, such as Breitbart news, and John Solomon's JustTheNews. On Fox I follow Sara Carter, check in on Sean Hannity and Tucker Carlson and Laura Ingram from time to time.

I really like Project Veritas and their undercover uncovering of the BS in the media and elsewhere. Then, because "know thy enemy" has its limits, when I want an attack of stomach cramps, I'll see what Jim Acaustic has to say on CNN.

I must mention the absolutely outstanding research work and articles by someone I have never met. The website is coreysdigs.com.

Corey's Digs has some excellent articles, and on one of her latest, I left this comment:- "As a 75-yr-old retired investigative journo and author myself, I have to say I have never seen such cogent factual reporting and depth of dot-connecting in my life." - Michael Knight.

The article concerned is at this link. (https://bit.ly/35EFFba)

My first visit to Corey's site was to an article titled "Shipwrecked on Ten Islands With Clinton and Branson." It is outstanding (htttps://bit.ly/3dolGjn)

While I could write a thousand words on each of the many ways in which evil hides behind good, this book has primarily been intended to bring you and other readers up to speed on what the Illuminati game plan has been.

It is not the definitive work on the whole subject. Rather, it is as much a research guide as it is a revelation of their intent, and an introduction to Q and the Qanon movement..

Therefore, you may wish to continue your research by taking up one or two of the following suggestions. Try using whatever keywords or phrases come to mind as you start using your search engine.
I use duckduckgo because it claims to make my searches anonymous. Google, as far as I am concerned, is a Deep State operation. They literally use algorithms to bury certain articles way past the first page, so you should keep that in mind and sometimes scroll through several pages.

Google also owns YouTube and just like Twitter and Facebook is banning many conservative channels and accounts.

Note too that any articles penned by the mainstream media, while worth reading to get their slant on the issue, are laced with half truths and spin. You'll often find that the headline is actually negated by the last few paragraphs.

Breitbart News, John Solomon, Sara Carter, Sharryl Attkisson and John Rappoport are genuine exceptions; honest researchers and "old school" ethics give their work real validity as far as I am concerned.

I believe we have all, me included, been naive in accepting at face value so much of what has passed for "news" over the years.

That's why it is so important to do your own checking and double checking, in order to see as much as possible of the big picture, who the players are, what their real intention might be, and why the media tends to work together to promote a narrative or focus on a particular "hot news" item – while buried in the back pages, so to speak, there is a paragraph or two about something truly significant that they do not want us to pay too much attention to.

Also, when visiting a website that you might not be familiar with, it's wise to check their "About" page and other site links.

This helps to determine whether or not they are legit, or possibly a Deep State asset. Beware too of satirical articles. The Babylon Bee makes no secret of the fact that it is pure satire, but even so, some people happily post some of their work as if it were gospel!

There are some truly bad writers out there. They write satire as if it is real news, and I have seen many on Facebook and Twitter repost or retweet spurious articles that show they have not bothered to try and find the source of what they are regurgitating.

By source, I mean you often come across a story that is reprinted and somewhat modified in the process. Therefore, it's essential to follow the credit link, if one is available, to the original author.

RESEARCH Q
A Starter List

Whatever subject you are researching, the basic questions almost always come down to *who, what, where, when* and *why?*

I am assuming for the purposes of this lesson that you'll primarily be looking for information related to Q, Qanons, the Deep State and how it operates.

If you are not yet familiar with the websites that Q posts on, the two I use most are **https://qanon.pub/?** and **https://qmap.pub/**.

Both have a topic search feature where you can call up over 4000 Q posts that have been dropped since October 2017. I'd recommend bookmarking those sites for quick access in future.

Many of Q's posts include a hyperlinked number in the first line which takes you to the original source. It might be a Twitter entry, or one of thousands of discussions on the main Q board where anonymous individuals (Qanons) from all over the world have their say.

You can also go directly to the Q research site (https://8kun.top/qresearch/index.html) or at **https://bit.ly/3bba3uT** if you wish to read posts by Qanons themselves, or if you may be thinking about joining those discussions yourself.

This starter list, in no particular order of importance, includes topics and suggested keywords, but of course you are free to choose your own as you go. (The plus (+) sign is not essential when inputting keywords or phrases).

Orientalreview.org. A variety of excellent articles looking at current international issues from different perspectives. (https://orientalreview.org/)

The Federal Reserve. When established. By whom? For what purpose? Keywords Fed+Trump+Treasury or Fed+Trump+Control. Also author G. Edward Griffin *"The Creature From, Jekyll Island."*

Allopathic medicine. Who started it in US? Conversely, deaths of homeopathic doctors. Keywords:- Rockefeller+Medicine

GMOs. Monsanto+glyphosate+Roundup and/or Monsanto+Court+Cases.

Red Cross. Red Cross+child+trafficking.

Clinton Foundation. Start with "crime against children" and try "Clinton Haiti" as well.

Charities. – Soros. McCain. Clinton. Gates. (Trey them one at a time).

NGOs. – Soros.
Soros – Diebold voting machines. Vote Fraud, BLM. Antifa.

Planned Parenthood. Eugenics. Organ harvesting. Bill Gates father past president.

DNA testing. (Why?)

Clones. Real or imagined? Cloned celebrities? Cloned politicians?

5G. Health issues. Understand the DSM only presents the pro-5G side of this story. I noted this particularly in a BBC interview April 30 2020 which hammered the theme that opponents are conspiracy theorists – but never deigned to interview any of them.

HIV AIDS. Not from a green monkey. San Francisco homosexuals injected with it under the guise of shots for Hepatitis B. That started the epidemic in the US, and has since killed off thousands of people worldwide.

Kids Drugs. Ritalin etc.

Drug trade. Vietnam and Afghanistan wars were both in some respects a cover for accessing and controlling the drug trade. Try colonel+bo+gritz.

Human trafficking. Arrests. Task Force. Statistics.

Subliminal advertising. To what purpose other than selling a product? To promote sexual deviancy perhaps?

Hollywood/Disney. What evidence of pedophilia and Satanic rituals? *"Disney is slated to openly embrace Hollywood's descent into the world of woke and feature its first openly lesbian character in its upcoming film Onward."*

Media conglomerates. How did thousands of media outlets in the US finish up being controlled by just six corporations? What do their symbols represent?

Google. What links to China and North Korea, and why?

United Nations. When founded. Main players? Real agenda?

Israel. When founded? By whom? For what purpose?

Pedophilia. Vatican. Catholic Church. Normalization. FBI arrests. John Podesta. Child sex abuse. Politicians and.

Satanic Rituals.
Bilderbergers.
Council on Foreign Relations.
Operation Mockingbird.
MKUltra. mind control.
Muslim Brotherhood. Huma Abedin. Valerie Jarrett. Obama administration.
Islam. Brennan. Obama.

Spygate. Fisagate. Pedogate. Pizzagate. Treason. Sub version. Obamagate.

And I'm sure you can think of a few more.

RECOMMENDED VIDEOS

One strategy in trying to red pill friends and family is to simply send them links to articles or videos that might help them get the message.

We all have email contacts, and some of them may be open to reading an article or watching a video where they wouldn't give you 30 seconds discussing the very same subjects.

I was particularly impressed with this first one because it is professionally made by two top Hollywood stuntmen whose eyes were opened to the point that they simply had to speak out.

Out Of Shadows. Posted April 10 2020 and over 11 million views in its first three weeks. "The Out Of The Shadows documentary lifts the mask on how the mainstream media & Hollywood manipulate & control the masses by spreading propaganda throughout their content. Our goal is to wake up the general public by shedding light on how we all have been lied to and brainwashed by a hidden enemy with a sinister agenda." Video at https://bit.ly/3ccWa0n

JFK to 911 Everything Is A Rich Man's Trick. Aaron Russo and Nicholas Rockefeller conversation – YouTube. https://bit.ly/3dqyki3

My YouTube Channel - North Star News. From "Clinton's Ghosts From Benghazi" to "Angels Beat Demons" and many more to choose from. All are Q-related and Trump supportive. https://bit.ly/2MKkxHR

Over 80 videos on Q-related subjects. (Subscribe to my free newsletter below for immediate notification of new ones, and exclusive articles.)

Documentary DVD by Michael Knight. Have you wondered why President Trump created the new Space Force? He (and Q) know more than they're telling us. (And from personal experience, I know more than I'm telling you:-) But this documentary I made was definitely ahead of its time. (ET) *Contact Has Begun* (Scroll down to view trailer) US sales only. http://bit.ly/UFOContactDVD

MK BOOKS AND VIDEOS

Book - *"President Trump and the New World Order – The Ramtha Trump Prophecy,"* **Reviews:-** *"Das Buch hat mir sehr gut gefallen"* (German = *"I liked the book very much."*0 ... *"One of the best books about the new world order and banking globalism."* ... *"This book is great, I bought 5 more to share with friends."* **Paperback Link** https://amzn.to/2Ruy3Co **Kindle Link** https://amzn.to/36xVkb1 .

Book - *"Qanon and the Great Awakening"* Reviews:- "I found this such an informative and enlightening read."…. "a rigorous, rugged portrayal of core aspects of societal control."... "I've read a few books on Q and this is the best to date." (https://amzn.to/37uOiVO)

My website shop page. Find numerous Q-related titles and books recommended by Q and/or President Trump, and books by other Qanon authors. http://bit.ly/2tUlG9P

Newsletter subscription Options. Paid version helps support ongoing work. Free version advises when new videos are uploaded, plus both will continue even if YT shuts down my channel. Subscribe to either one at this link. Scroll down to free one. https://northstarnewsletter.com

My Patreon Site. My Patrons have been a great help in covering costs associated with this work. I myself am a patron of several other Q-related Patreon sites, such as Coreysdigs, Martin Geddes, and Qappanon.

They all spend countless hours using their particular skills for the benefit of others. None of us is "in it for the money." (But it certainly helps us keep going.)

The vast majority of people get everything we do for free and there's no begrudging that. Just helping The Great Awakening is a reward in iutself.

However, there are overheads, and there are people who are warmhearted and do have the wherewithal to become patrons (for as little as $3 a month) which is deeply appreciated (https://bit.ly/3bpJ66J).

REVIEWS – PLEASE

Y our review is important – especially for those who are searching for an understanding of why the world is in such a bad state and what to expect for the future.

If you are a verified buyer from Amazon, the following link makes it easy to go straight to the review page; although as a heads up you will be asked to log in. Please do – and believe me, I look forward to reading your review. Amazon.com/review/create-review?&asin=ISBN: 978-1-7340837-4-3

If that doesn't work, please try the old-fashioned way. Just find the book on Amazon and look for the reviews and then, gitter-done:-)

ABOUT THE AUTHOR

Starting in New Zealand in 1960 I spent several decades working as a reporter, editor, newsreader, Tv reporter and documentary maker etc. in all branches of the media.

I have lived in America since 1990, but before that I had lived and worked or covered assignments in Australia, Britain, the UK, Canada and the United States.

Truth be told, I became a reporter because writing was my passion, but as a teenager I knew I had no real life experience to write about, and no desire to become a starving author.

Journalism allowed me to get paid for writing, to travel at my employers' expense, meet thousands of people around the world, master various media skills from newspapers to radio and television.

I was twice awarded the Hoben Prize for Journalism when working for The Taranaki Daily News, New Plymouth, New Zealand. While working for that newspaper I volunteered to go to Vietnam as a correspondent for the New Zealand Press Association. The assignment was canceled when the NZPA opted to get its reports from Reuters. I later missed the draft by a day. Thank God – and all his friends.

In 1969 I was recruited by Hamersley Iron to be Assistant Public Relations Manager at their iron ore mining endeavor in Western Australia, and from there moved to Perth as a radio newsreader for TVW7/6IX.

I returned to New Zealand and established my own PR company, working on contract as a reporter, while my company also produced international marketing films. Television New Zealand split into two channels – which in hindsight now looks to have had the fingerprint of the Globalists all over it - but it doubled the demand for news camera crews. I took advantage of that by setting up two crews to work on a pay-per-assignment basis.

That in turn gave me hands-on experience as a news cameraman. (It's interesting how objective or "distant" you can become when seeing the world through the lens of a camera.)

Aside from journalism I have also written a few short stories and was once placed second in a national NZ short story competition – reminiscing about a truly death defying flight out of Breaksea Sound over the Southern Alps with a drunken helicopter pilot.

Talk about the benefit of seeing the world through the lens of an 8mm camera...

My first book, co-authored with my then partner Liz Brook, was *"Building With Logs In New Zealand."* It sold out in New Zealand, Canada and the US.

I later co-authored a rewrite of *"Playboys of the South Pacific,"* with John Glennie, who had survived 119 days adrift in the Pacific in his upturned trimaran.

While doing a stint as Economics Reporter for Television New Zealand in the 70s, I became somewhat aware of the Cabal thanks to a book titled *"The Unseen Hand."*

But now, some 40 years later, I have seen firsthand how the

media can be infiltrated by "reporters" with connections to intelligence agencies such as Britain's MI5 and MI6 and the CIA; agencies which I have only recently discovered are themselves controlled by the secret powers above.

I believe in the Constitution of the United States of America, and the Bill of Rights.

I also know without a doubt that unless I ally myself with the millions of patriots who see what is happening, and do what I can to unmask the pariahs that have infiltrated this country – and the world - the freedoms my father fought to preserve will most certainly be destroyed by the likes of the Globalists and corrupt politicians, and my father's service will have been in vain.

My father loaded bombs and bullets. I prefer a loaded pen.
- *Michael Knight, May 13 2020.*

CONTACT MICHAEL KNIGHT

email - contact@northstarnewsletter.com

Please use "Feedback" in the Subject Line.

All will be read but cannot guarantee a response. Selected content may be used for marketing purposes, using only the initials of the sender.

ADDENDUM – THE VIRUS SPEAKS

Corona's Letter To Humanity

The earth whispered but you did not hear.
The earth spoke but you did not listen
The earth screamed but you turned her off.

And so I was born...

I was not born to punish you..
I was born to awaken you..

The earth cried out for help...

Massive flooding. But you didn't listen.
Burning fires. But you didn't listen.
Strong hurricanes. But you didn't listen.
Terrifying Tornadoes. But you didn't listen.

You still don't listen to the earth when.

Ocean animals are dying due to pollutants in the waters.
Glaciers melting at an alarming rate.
Severe drought.

You didn't listen to how much negativity
the earth is receiving.

Non-stop wars.
Non-stop greed.

You just kept going on with your life..

No matter how much hate there was..
No matter how many killings daily..

It was more important to get that latest iPhone than
worry about what the earth was trying to tell you..

But now I am here.

And I've made the world stop on its tracks.

I've made YOU finally listen.
I've made you take refuge.
I've made you stop thinking about materialistic things..

Now you are like the earth...

You are only worried about YOUR survival.

How does that feel?

I give you fever.. as the fires burn on earth.
I give you respiratory issues.. as your pollution
filled the earth air.

I gave you weakness as the earth weakens every day.

I took away your comforts..
Your outings.
The things you would use to forget
about the planet and its pain.

And I made the world stop...

And now...
China has better air quality..
Skies are clear blue because factories are not
spewing pollution unto the earth's air.

The water in Venice is clean and dolphins are
being seen. Because the gondola boats that
pollute the water are not being used.

YOU are having to take time to reflect on
what is important in your life.

Again I am not here to punish you.. I
am here to Awaken you...

When all this is over and I am gone... Please
remember these moments..

Listen to the earth.
Listen to your soul.
Stop Polluting the earth.
Stop Fighting among each other.
Stop caring about materialistic things.
And start loving your neighbours.
Start caring about the earth and all its creatures.
Start believing in a Creator.

Because next time, I may come back even stronger....

Signed,
Corona – The Virus

(Author Unknown).

Made in the USA
Coppell, TX
03 July 2020